Designing Rituals
of Adoption

for the Religious and Secular Community

by Mary Martin Mason
edited by Daryl Parks

This publication was made possible
by a grant from:
The United States Department of Health and Human Services
awarded to RAP - Resources for Adoptive Parents
#90-CO-0636 entitled
"SELECT Program for Preservation of Special Needs Adoption"

RAP - RESOURCES FOR ADOPTIVE PARENTS
3381 Gorham Avenue
Minneapolis, Minnesota 55426

Designing Rituals of Adoption for the Religious and Secular Community

Published by RAP—Resources for Adoptive Parents
3381 Gorham Avenue
Minneapolis, Minnesota 55426

Designed by Jodee Kulp
Better Endings New Beginnings
119 North Fourth Street, Suite 401
Minneapolis, Minnesota 55401
(612) 341-9870 Facsimile (612) 337-5104

Alternative Cataloging - in - Publication Data

Mason, Mary Martin

   Designing Rituals of Adoption for the Religious and Secular Community.

Minneapolis, Minnesota: RAP—Resources for Adoptive Parents, copyright 1995.

   PARTIAL CONTENTS: Jewish adoption rituals. —Christian adoption

rituals. —Ecumenical services of adoptions. —Secular rituals. —Gifts. —Bibliography. —Ethnic recipes.

   —Other helpful resources.

   ISBN 0-9646259-0-3

   1. Adoption rituals. I. Title. II. Title: Rituals of adoption for the religious and secular community.

   III. Title: Adoption rituals for the religious and secular community.

   IV. RAP—Resources for Adoptive Parents.

362.734

Our heartfelt thanks go to...

RAP - Resources for Adoptive Parents' Rituals in Adoption Committee who worked tirelessly to coordinate concepts, contact resource people and design adoption rituals. The committee was led by Holly van Gulden and was comprised of:

>Janis Dehler
>Mary Martin Mason
>Penny Needham
>Claude Riedel

RAP also appreciates the contributions of:

>Judge Philip Busch
>Rabbi Norman Cohen
>Cheryl Flugaur-Leavitt
>Reverend Robert Foltz-Morrison
>Pastor Luis Gonzales
>Karen Harrison-Hatchell
>Reverend Vivian Jones
>Linda Kuhlmann
>Jodee Kulp Graphic Arts
>Laurie Larsen
>Joan McNamara
>Peggy Meyer
>Reverend Susan Milnor
>Karen O'Connel, Congregations Concerned for Children
>Daryl Parks
>Father Tim Powers
>Laurel Riedel
>Gary B. Rierson, Minneapolis Council of Churches
>Father Vincent Schwann
>Caroline Stevens
>Father Allen Russell Tilsen
>Lois Vetvick
>Peg Wagenstein, Congregations Concerned for Children

Also by the Author

Mary Martin Mason
The Miracle Seekers: An Anthology of Infertility
Our of the Shadows: Birthfathers' Stories

Also by the Book Designer

Jodee Kulp
Journey To Life
Families at Risk: A Guide to Understanding and Protecting Children
and Care Providers Involved in Out-of-Home or Adoptive Care

Contents

"People not presently involved with a traditional religion deserve access to safe and life-affirming ritual methods with which they can feel comfortable. Those within religious or spiritual traditions can benefit by a more conscious understanding of the rituals they utilize. Both can benefit by bringing awareness and intention to the secular rituals that are a regular part of life." [1]

Renee Beck, *The Art of Ritual*

1   Renee Beck, <u>The Art of Ritual</u> (Berkeley, California: Celestial Arts, 1990), 10.

Introduction

The purpose of this booklet is to design rituals which recognize the life passages and life transitions which are unique within adoption, the most common being:

— *a child leaving his/her birth family and joining an adoptive family.*

— *birthparents relinquishing their role as parents and seeking peace with that decision.*

— *adoptive parents assuming their role as parents and honoring and/or acknowledging birthparents who may be known or unknown.*

In the religious community:

— *the congregation, serving as witnesses who bless and support this life passage.*

— *the priest, rabbi or minister offering a blessing on the child, as well as the birth family and adoptive family members.*

In the secular community:

— *Participants expressing their respective part in this translation through music, symbolic acts, prepared or extemporaneous words and/or readings.*

Many of the symbolic acts and inclusions found in the section on Secular Adoption Rituals may be applicable to religious adoption rituals. Particularly helpful is a guide to planning and designing rituals that is found in that section.

Why Rituals?
Why Adoption Rituals?

"From the exchange of wedding bands to the recitation of prayers for the dead, rituals mark transitions in family life and help families heal. They create change as well as create an awareness of change, provide a vehicle for people to express their feelings, define relationships, help arrive at solutions and restore balance to lives that have been disrupted by change or crisis." [2]

Lois Ruskai Melina and Sharon Kaplan Roszia

For many years adoption has neither been celebrated nor ritualized. The practicing philosophy was "Take the baby home and act as if he or she were born to you." When adoption issues surfaced, they were ignored or attributed to some other cause. Today we accept the unique aspects of adoption, not the least of which is that a child who is adopted has two families and will face some identity issues which revolve around that fact. Research and practice have shown that acknowledging the differences in adoption helps everyone involved to be healthier.

All rituals are centered around transitions which are comprised of beginnings, endings, cycles and healing. Even a wedding includes all of these elements: the beginning of a shared life, the ending of being single and of the relationship as it was practiced with one's parents, the cycle of adulthood and perhaps the beginning of a family. Healing is a component of the wedding ceremony, acknowledging in the wedding vows that the future may hold adversity through which the individuals must work individually and together. In many ways an adoption ritual mirrors a wedding ritual. For the participants, the ritual acknowledges:

— *the beginning or the formation of the adoptive family,*

— *the ending of the birthparents' role as acting parents and for a child who has been in foster homes, the ending of impermanence as a family member.*

— *the cycle of adoption as a part of life's journey, or in cases of repeated adoption rituals, the cycle will indicate where various persons are within their individual journey, and*

— *the healing which will address the loss in adoption which needs to be given credence.*

---

2   Lois Ruskai Melina and Sharon Kaplan Roszia, <u>The Open Adoption Experience</u> (New York: Harper Perennial, 1993), 133.

Like a pebble dropped into the water, the transition of a child into his/her adoptive family ripples through and transforms many lives. The child's birth or foster parents will no longer nurture that child. If contact is not maintained between the various families, the birthparents' extended family may no longer be able to claim the role of aunt, uncle, cousin, sibling or grandparent. A birthmother's older children may watch their connection dissolve with their sibling and wonder if their relationship to her is still intact. Instead, the adoptive parents will now assume the role of legal, emotional and physical parents to a child who was not born to them.

The adopted child is profoundly affected by this transition. Not only is the child's future altered, but his or her past may no longer be accessible. Along with different physical surroundings and a new name will come unfamiliar sounds, tastes, smells and sights. The family may bring changes in the child's cultural heritage, religion, customs, expectations and social status.

Cultures have distinctive rituals which assign meaning to life transitions and define membership within that particular culture. Tribes, clans and ethnic groups throughout the world use rituals and ceremonies to designate a child's birth, coming of age, marriage, new parenthood and dying.

While few Westerners can explain why a bride wears objects which are borrowed, blue, old and new, many ethnic groups can trace their rituals to myths, stories and truths which have been passed down generation to generation. Native Americans rely on elders, sometimes called Wisdom-keepers, to teach them dances, drumming and chanting associated with cycles of life, healing and planting. Families may design or create costumes for dancers or present them with an eagle feather or other sacred objects to use during a particular ritual.

A name is the strongest symbol of identity for a person. Westerners typically name a child according to popularity and style. "Johnny" and "Debbie" will be the choice of one generation, while "Zack" and "Zoe" the choice of another.

Many cultures recognize the power of a name and thus design rituals around names. For instance, in Tibet each baby is given a secret name by a Buddhist lama as well as a public name. The secret name is worn on a pouch around the neck for life. In Viet Nam, some fathers name the sons while mothers name the girls. Jewish children are traditionally named after a deceased relative.

Whether naming their child or moving into a new passage in life, Westerners typically have more difficulty designing rituals than non-Western cultures and native peoples. Our culture has been trained to respect science over abstract thinking, to practice actions instead of to examine feelings, and in a time of crisis, to seek a logical, quick solution.

The few rituals that we do perform contain the thread of family participation because family members are an integral and important part of our lives. A father and/or mother may walk a daughter down the aisle on her wedding day. Siblings or in-laws may serve as godparents in a christening, Brit Milah or naming ceremony for a girl. Relatives may be pall bearers at a funeral.

The celebration of a bar or bat mitzvah is a unique ceremony in which a Jewish boy or girl is accepted into the congregation. Since the ceremony represents the entrance into adulthood, the child may be the sole participant. Siblings and parents may read from the Torah and participate to varying degrees depending on Orthodox, Conservative or Reform Jewish traditions. Even though the boy or girl will be the focus of the ritual, the family's presence is always profoundly felt during the ceremony and at the celebration afterwards.

Adoption presents the unique situation of a baby or older child leaving his/her family of origin to join another family. Families that are not biologically connected will be intertwined through the child, whether or not they meet one another. As a common thread, "family" is complex for everyone involved. Each person who is tied by a thread to this baby or older child will need a ceremony to mark the simultaneous end and beginning that will occur.

Each participant who takes part in the ritual marks his/her place in the adoption and unravels his/her piece of the common thread. Inclusion of birthparents, either by attendance or by proxy, affirms their decision at the beginning of this adoption, releases their role as acting parents, and emphasizes their unbreakable, genetic connection to the child. Adoptive parents receive empowerment and validation for their new roles. For children, rather than being caught between fantasies about their birthparents and examining where they fit in the adoptive family, the ritual reveals where they began and also where they now belong.

Special attention needs to be given to all adopted children. Older children may need to show and be shown ritualistically that their adoption is not a temporary arrangement, especially if they have been moved repeatedly throughout the foster care system. Younger children and infants who will not remember the ceremony or ritual may some day view it on videotape, see photographs or hear family accounts of this event. For them, the ritual becomes more than a public record; it will be an integral part of their life chronicle.

In international adoptions it is vitally important to recognize the child's heritage in the ritual. Symbols, music, articles of clothing, foods and/or traditions from the child's native country do more than add flavor to the ceremony; instead, they mark the child's ethnicity, recognize his/her dual community membership and pay tribute to his/her family and country of origin.

The transition into adoption should be made meaningful for each participant through the development of ceremonies which appropriately validate the event. The child's age, culture and race, stage of development (if the child is not an infant) and history should be incorporated into the transference. A blending of the child's genetic/cultural heritage and the adoptive family's composition and history will be important in establishing the foundation for a successful beginning.

This book deals primarily with transference ceremonies which are called Entrustment or Welcoming Ceremonies. Entrustment and Welcoming Ceremonies ritualize the actual movement of a child from one family to another. Even when the two families have never met, birthparents can be a symbolic part of the ceremony or they may be represented by proxy. The focal point of the ritual is the child and his or her passage into adoption.

Religious Rites:
Why Invent Tradition?

Religious rules prescribe a pre-determined way to perform a ritual through a ceremony, act, observance or procedure which is called a rite. The base of most rituals is tradition. Faith rituals are built on religious traditions. Rituals outside the religious community are based on seeking enlightenment in ways that may not fall within religious parameters. (See Secular Rituals on page 47.)

Some clergy and congregations may pose questions about creating new adoption rites. They may ask, "Doesn't our church or synagogue already have these in place? Won't the religious rites and ceremonies designated for families and for children fit adoptive families and adopted children as well?"

Perhaps the best answer can be given by example. A christening was scheduled into a regular worship service. The baby was Korean and the parents were white, but no mention was made of adoption. An elderly man was heard to mutter his confusion from a back pew, "I know it must be an adoption, but why doesn't anybody say so?" For him and for other congregants, the double-bind message is: there are some unique elements in this ritual that separate it from other christenings, and yet no one chooses to acknowledge them. By not speaking about the child's beginnings, a gap is created in the substance and content of the ritual.

Brit Milah is the traditional Jewish ceremony for a baby boy. Although the adoptive father may easily recite the blessing reserved for a father, the rabbi may not wish to give the blessing which is translated, "May the father be happy with the offspring of his loins and the mother rejoice with the fruit of her womb."[3] Obviously reserved for the biological parents, the happy blessing is also not appropriate to attribute to the grieving birthparents.

In her wedding a perplexed bride struggles with the quandary of who should step forward to "give her away." Recently reunited with her birthmother, her adoptive father now deceased, she is dissatisfied with her priest's advice: "Of course your mother who raised you should be the one. Not only is it traditional. It's correct!" For the bride, the issue goes beyond tradition and correctness. Until she had met her birthmother and heard firsthand of the circumstances that had led to her adoption, this bride had often felt "given away." Now, at this important juncture in her life, the phrase still holds sadness as well as a divided loyalty to two women, one who has given her physical life and the other who she calls Mom.

Adoption is one of the few familial transitions that is overlooked by both the lay and religious communities. Religious exclusion of adoption reference and adoption language can result in adoptive and birth families feeling unsupported and invalidated within their church or synagogue.

---

3   Proverbs 23:25. This blessing, although taking a variety of translations, is an integral part of the Brit Milah service in all branches of Judaism.

To understand why this exclusion is significant, the purpose of rituals must be examined.

Rituals:

— *Mark and define us, either by our relationship to God or by our place in the world and among the people around us.*

— *Comprise our habits in everyday life (fixing coffee and having a bagel upon waking in the morning) and thus comprise the fabric of our being.*

— *Let us know where we are inside our life's journey, marking important life and death passages/transitions.*

— *Connect us to those who came before us and those who will come after us.*

— *Provide, define and display membership or inter-reliance within a community which may be religious, familial or as large a group as the human family.*

— *Create understanding and support among those who participate or who serve as witnesses to the ritual.*

Therapeutic Rituals

This is the Hour of Lead -
Remembered, if outlived,
As Freezing persons, recollect the Snow -
First - Chill - then Stupor - then the letting go -
Emily Dickinson

Long before therapists became a mainstay in our culture, rituals provided healing to ancient peoples. With or without guidance from a spiritual leader, humans have found ways to ritualistically contain their grief. That practice continues today both inside and outside of organized religion.

These days, rituals are used as therapy, helping participants name unspeakable sorrow through designing and performing a ritual. Therapeutic rituals are appropriate and can bring about healing in a number of settings. Some clergy, spiritual leaders and professionals who serve the adoption community will wish to provide guidance and/or give permission to those who need to invent a healing ritual.

For instance, a birthmother learns that the baby she relinquished died as a teenager. Although the funeral and burial were performed many years ago, she needs a memorial service to hold and mark her grief. The ceremony will include symbols and objects that are symbolic of the child she never knew. Photographs of the newborn child, a rattle or blanket that was touched by the baby or footprints taken in the hospital may serve this purpose. The rite will either be public or private and may either include or not include the adoptive family.

Birthparents need a symbolic way to celebrate the birth of their child while releasing them. They will choose to keep something which represents their children, be it flowers, rocks, jewelry or a keepsake. They can then design a ritual around that object. Sister Jose Hobday, a Franciscan nun, suggests "letting go" by transferring grief to a flower which is sacrificed. [4]

Another example of a therapeutic ritual concerns those children who have suffered abuse or neglect or who may have been in multiple foster care homes. The children need a way to understand that the connection with their adoptive parents is different than the stays with foster families or birth families. Similarly, the family members want a way to show their permanent commitment to one another. Therapist Claudia Jewett has devised a ritual in which candles are lit to symbolize each "holding place" in which the children had stayed.[5] The candles representing the abusive homes are snuffed out, the candles representing the supportive homes are kept burning, and the adoptive family's candle burns brightest and longest.

Therapist, Joan McNamara says that rituals are excellent tools for adults to use in helping children make sense of life. She also says that if children are stuck in the early stages of grieving such as denial or anger, they will not be able to understand lighting a candle or other symbolism. This does not mean that the ritual shouldn't be done, but that other rituals should be considered, or interim steps need to occur within the child's developmental stage. She also suggests repeating rituals in a timely fashion, according to the needs of the child.

Adoption Rituals Can be Teaching Tools

Many rituals are performed publicly so that witnesses can offer support to the participants. In return for attending the ritual, the guests indirectly take part. For that reason we may cry at a wedding, mourn at a funeral, smile sweetly at a christening or recall our youth at the celebration of a bar or bat mitzvah.

More importantly, rituals are reminders of our own place in time. At weddings we are reminded of our own vows, at funerals we are reminded of our mortality, at birth and adoption rituals we are reminded of the relationships and commitment that come with family. Each reminder allows us to bless the participants.

In religious settings, either Jewish or Christian, most congregations learn about adoption solely through scriptural reference. In the Old Testament, Moses was adopted by the pharaoh's daughter and Queen Esther was adopted by her uncle, Mordecai. Rabbinic literature describes the Jewish sacred relationship to God through God adopting David, legitimizing God's dynasty and showing how God adopts the people of Israel as God's own. [6]

---

4   See Page 67
5   Claudia Jewett. Adopting the Older Child. (Harvard, Massachusetts: Harvard Common Press, 1978), 113.
6   Jeremiah 3:19, 31:8. Hosea 11:1

Christian doctrine emphasizes that through faith in Christ, Christians are adopted by God into the church.[7] Other than these examples, adoption is rarely included in liturgy and almost never acknowledged through rituals.

In secular and public settings, adoption is laden with stereotypes. Those who have never had contact with adoption view it from a media-hype viewpoint, such as the Baby Jessica case or the bitter custody fights between Mia Farrow and Woody Allen. Birthparents who appear on talk shows are viewed as uncaring, unprincipled persons. School teachers, clergy and health professionals often consider adopted persons to have fragile backgrounds and thus are more likely to have troubled futures. Adoptive parents encounter such myths as "blood is thicker than water" and "you could never love a child not born to you as much as you could your biological child."

Those who attend an adoption ritual receive information which overcomes stereotypes and lets them know what the participants may need from them, including:

— *A transracial adoption instantly announces a child's family history before he or she has the option to do so. Sometimes called a "fishbowl adoption," the difference in the child and parents' races broadcasts personal information which might not be stated in other circumstances. Being sensitive to transracial issues is vital.*

— *Parents who adopt children with special needs are not saints, but caring individuals who need occasional respite from constant childcare, as all parents do.*

— *Birthparents make a life-altering, selfless decision and will always care about their birth child. They can feel and display grief at the same time that they affirm adoption as being their choice for the child.*

— *For adopted persons, reunions provide many answers to "who am I?" Connecting with birthparents does not dissolve the adopted person's connection to their adoptive parents, but may actually strengthen and validate that connection.*

Specific rituals are needed to commemorate the transition of a child through adoption. One minister put it this way: "In adoption, relationships begin to take a totally different form and content."

In the sections to follow, "welcoming" rituals from various religions are included with suggestions for the inclusion of adoption. Several charts are given from which families may select appropriate liturgy or symbolic actions to create their own ritual.

Matters of faith are highly personal, connecting us with those who share our faith and sometimes separating us from those who don't. Because this book addresses both Judeo-Christian[8] and secular issues, it is sure to offend some reader's spiritual sensibilities. Readers should always consult their rabbi, priest, minister or spiritual leader, conscience and individual beliefs when designing a religious ritual.

---

7   Ephesians 1:5

8   Space restrictions in this book do not allow for covering religious viewpoints other than Judaism and Christianity. Many of the principles covered may be applied to other forms of spirituality and religions.

What about Open Adoption?

*"Adoption is almost always framed as a zero-sum equation -
one mother's loss becomes another's boon. For this family, the
terms are not so simple. Everyone celebrates; everyone's
scared; everyone survives. When it is Simon's (the adopted
child) turn to assemble a life, all the complex pieces of his
past will be there, waiting."*

Anndee Hochman[9]

Following decades of secrecy and of closed birth records for adopted persons, open adoption is growing in practice among birth and adoptive families. In open adoption, after a face-to-face meeting, the parties design an adoption which may include ongoing contact through a wide variety of models. The child participates by having contact with his or her birth family.

In semi-open adoption, the birth and adoptive family may or may not have had a face-to-face meeting. Typically they do not know each other's last names or identifying information such as addresses. Participants stay in touch using an intermediary such as an adoption agency, lawyer or adoption facilitator. The intermediary passes non-identifying information such as pictures and updates on the child from family to family.

An obvious result of blending birth and adoptive families is that the adoption ritual will encompass celebration and sadness. Since adoption begins with the birthparents' relinquishment of the child, it is appropriate to acknowledge their loss as a piece of this life-altering event. Sometimes the participants can address this loss in bonding ways. Randolph Severson describes an Adoption Placement Ceremony in which an adoptive mother, holding her child in her arms, asked the birthmother if they could pray together. She said, "Dear Lord, who has blessed my family today with a joy and love that truly is surpassing, bless this woman, too, for though I cannot understand your pain, your grief at having to give away this child, God in his infinite wisdom knows it, shares it, feels it, and I hope I can feel it someday, too. I know he will heal us both and in healing us, heal our child who is not really our child at all but who is his, whom he gives to us because he loves us, as we must learn to love one another." [10]

No statistics exist that reflect how many birthparents and adoptive parents are of the same or different religions. In an open adoption when there is not a religious match, the ritual can be ecumenical and thus acknowledge the faiths of the various participants. Just as in a wedding, careful discussion and planning in adoption rituals should occur before blending ecumenical elements. Since religion is very personal, the potential for offending someone during an ecumenical ritual is more pronounced.

---

9 Anndee Hochman, <u>Everyday Acts and Small Subversions</u> (Portland, Oregon: Eighth Mountain Press, 1994), 122.

10 Randolph W. Severson. <u>Eyes that Shine: Essays on Open Adoption.</u> (Dallas, Texas: House of Tomorrow Productions, 1992), 26.

The Entrustment Ceremony[11]

As adoption practices evolve into more open arrangements, rituals that blend adoptive and birth families are being designed to mark the time when a child leaves one family to join the other. Often called an Entrustment Ceremony, the rite provides a way for adoptive and birth families to celebrate their joys, clarify their new roles and mark their sorrows. Depending on the degree of contact between birthparents and adoptive parents, an Entrustment Ceremony may include participants either by proxy or in person.

Entrustment Ceremonies are becoming more common in hospitals as a fitting way to transfer the baby from the birth family to the adoptive family. In the past, this awkward and sometimes public transference has taken place in the hospital parking lot or under the watchful eye of hospital personnel. An Entrustment Ceremony provides a way for birthparents and their extended families to say goodbye and not feel that they are abandoning their child.

As with other rituals, an Entrustment Ceremony offers clergy the opportunity to educate their congregations about a life passage which is centered in faith. At first, congregations may be amazed that birthparents and adoptive parents can share in this ritual (if they are comfortable) and that birthparents can be publicly mentioned and honored for their integral part of adoption. The ritual will feel incomplete unless the acts of the birthparents giving and the adoptive parents receiving are symbolically or physically included.

In cases of transracial adoptions, the Entrustment Ceremony should include mention of the child's cultural, ethnic and racial heritage. Symbols, music and readings or prayers in the child's native language can be valuable additions to the ritual as well. On page 36-40, a New Zealand service of "Thanksgiving for the Gift of a Child" can be found in its entirety. This beautiful service is mindful of birthparents and of the native people of New Zealand (including a prayer and blessing in Maori) and thus provides a valuable guide for families and clergy who are creating rituals honoring a child's ethnicity.

If the Entrustment Ceremony is religious, the Biblical story of Hannah, found in First Samuel 1:9-18, has application for both birth and adoptive parents. The grief of infertility is represented in Hannah, "a woman of sorrowful spirit" who speaks the bitterness she feels in her heart. That bitterness dissolves into a vow which expresses the sacrifice that birthparents make in adoption; Hannah will give her child to the Lord. Eli's first blessing applies to both adoptive and birth families: "Go in peace, and the God of Israel grant thee thy petition that thou hast asked of him." The final verse presents the hope of peace and resolution for birthparents: "And she said, 'Let thine handmaid find grace in thy sight.' So the woman went her way, and did eat, and her countenance was no more sad."

---

11   Lois Ruskai Melina and Sharon Kaplan Roszia. The Open Adoption Experience. (New York: Harper Perennial, 1993). 133.

If the ritual is not religious, birthparent(s) can be included in symbolic actions, lighting a candle with adoptive parents, sharing in readings of poetry, preparing a joint family tree with the birthparents' family as the roots and the adoptive family as the branches. A secular section in the book has suggestions for non-religious entrustment ceremonies.

The focal point of the Entrustment Ceremony occurs when the birthparent(s) hand the child to the adoptive parents. Not only is this action symbolic of the transfer of parental title and role, but it provides a way for each family to give and receive the child, which is the essence of an Entrustment Ceremony. Some closure is provided for birthparent(s), allowing them to move on with their healing.

Following an Entrustment Ceremony one birthmother said, "I realize that even if I have a child in the future, I cannot replace Danny. Handing him to Rick and Kathy was the hardest, saddest, best thing I've ever done."

If birthparent(s) are missing but are represented by proxy, the entrustment can still be accomplished. The proxy birthparents who physically exchange the child with the adoptive parents are doing more than going through the motions. Their act is symbolic of the decision of the birthparents and represents their care and thoughtful planning, albeit in abstentia.

Some birthparents write a letter which states the reason they chose adoption for their child. If such a letter is in the possession of the adoptive parents, they may read that letter at the Entrustment Ceremony in lieu of the birthparent(s) being able to speak in person.

Ritualizing the
Adoption Finalization Ceremony

During an adoption finalization, each county and state has prescribed questions that are asked of adoptive parent(s) and a process which is recorded by a court recorder. Even so, the adoption finalization need not be a cold formality.

While time and staffing restraints of a court calendar would make it difficult to plan a lengthy ceremony, according to Judge Phillip Busch, most judges would agree to an augmented ceremony or ritual as long as the lines between the secular and non-secular are clear. The constitutional separation of church and state requires that boundaries must be kept between religion and the court.

Just as for weddings, it is possible to hire a judge and a court reporter during off hours to travel to a private setting. A judge who knows the participants personally might be more willing to accommodate this request. Most judges enjoy performing adoption finalizations and might be inclined to participate in a private family ceremony following the formal court process.

Judges today are increasingly exposed to open, mediated and designated adoptions where birthparents have met and/or selected the adoptive parents. Although the legal process in most states is still being driven by the older model of private/closed adoption, birthparents may legally be included in the finalization, if all the participants are comfortable doing so.

A finalization ritual can be very important to an older child who has the cognitive ability to grasp the concept of permanency. Adoption changes the blueprint of previous arrangements, so the ritual needs to clearly say, "This is different. This is a commitment from the family and from the community to support your forever family."

Holly van Gulden, a therapist who has created and performed many finalization rituals for older children, sees marked changes in the child after the finalization ritual. The changes may be immediate or may develop over time as a child processes the ritual. Van Gulden said, "The ritual really solidifies changing the pattern of how foster children have moved from place to place. All the previous moves have been temporary stays. One child got very nervous but was relieved by the ritual at the same time. He said that being in foster care was like pulling into a Greyhound Bus Station. During the ritual he said, 'Wait a minute. I'm not taking the next bus out.'"

Adding vows in the adoption ritual of the older child may increase the ritual's significance. Patterned after the wedding ceremony, adoptive parents can swear to provide permanence, love and care to their new son or daughter. The child, in turn, can vow to be a member of their new family and to take this man and/or woman as Mom and/or Dad. Other family members, who will need to be integrated into this enlarged family, may also make vows. Language from the traditional wedding ceremony can be used such as "in sickness and in health" or modernized as in, "I accept you for now and for the future." A candle of unity can be lit to represent the newly formed family.

One child who went through such a ceremony said of her adoption finalization, "That was the day officially that I adopted them, and they adopted me before God and the judge." This child's understanding of her place in her family is affixed. For a child who has been in multiple homes, it is important that their passage into their adoptive family be marked and articulated. Otherwise it will feel very much like other moves they may have made through "the system."

The Religious Adoption Ceremony

"Ritual - a coherent set of symbolic actions that has a real, transformative effect on individuals and small groups."[12]

Some common elements in a religious ritual which may be included in an adoption Entrustment, Welcoming or Naming Ceremony or Thanksgiving for the Gift/Adoption of a Child,[13] regardless of the religion, are:

— *A setting such as a church or synagogue, home, chapel at a hospital or in a place that holds special meaning for the participants.*

— *A leader or celebrant such as a priest, minister or rabbi.*

— *By their presence, witnesses validate and express their support for this transition, learn from it and define membership within their community incorporating the newly formed family.*

— *Witnesses acknowledge the birth family's loss (if they are present), offer them support and help them bring closure to the relinquishment of their role as day-to-day parents.*

— *Appropriate readings from the Torah and Tanahk, or from the Bible, perhaps read by birth and adoptive family members.*

— *Gifts that are exchanged between families or presented to the child by participants.*

— *Sacred or secular music that is meaningful to the participants.*

— *Symbolic actions that suggest meaning beyond the present moment.*

— *The reciting of names of participants. If some participants are not present, mention them by their role in the ritual or have them be represented by proxy.*

— *A blessing that is given by the celebrant and/or by the witnesses for the child and his/her birth and adoptive families.*

---

12   Bruce Lincoln. Emerging from the Chrysalis: Studies in Rituals in Women's Initiations, (Cambridge, Massachusetts: Harvard University, 1981), 6.

13   A Thanksgiving for the Gift/Adoption of a Child is a service designed for giving thanks and beginning and sealing family life.

JEWISH ADOPTION RITUALS

"My mother has this theory of celebrating every event, like it's a law. I think she's right. It's important to acknowledge these things. You never know if you're going to be around for the next one; you never know how many people are going to be around for the next one. You invite who's alive. You do what you can do."

Roberta Lampert speaks about her daughter's Naming Ceremony[14]

A rabbi friend who shared his vast library for the writing of this book, offered this advice: "What you are doing is breaking tradition," he said. "But in a way, adoption also breaks tradition, so perhaps it is appropriate."

When the rabbi spoke of adoption as breaking tradition, he was not being negative but rather was addressing what it means to be Jewish. Except in cases of conversion, Judaism is based on lineage through birth family, regardless of adoption status. Therefore, a child whose birthfather is a Kohen or a Levite will retain that status, but a child whose adoptive father is a Kohen or a Levite will not be treated as such. Many Jewish rituals are rooted in lineage, such as reciting a Kaddish or having a Pidyon Haben. In adoption, determining how or if such rituals can be performed will depend on Reform, Conservative or Orthodox Jewish tradition within one's synagogue.

One of the first considerations in designing an adoption ceremony is Brit. Brit is the Hebrew word for covenant. One of God's "Brits" to Abraham and his descendants is the promise of his commitment to them. Incorporating a child into the brit is accomplished through the Brit Milah for a boy and Simhat Bat for a girl.

Although an Entrustment Ceremony may contain elements of a brit, the ritual should focus on the transfer of the child from his/her birth family into his/her adoptive family. Witnessing this ceremony may help the congregation to understand and support that passage. A ritual may also help them bridge, but not dismiss the many theological questions about the status of a gentile-born child who is adopted into a Jewish family.

---

14   Anndee Hochman, <u>Everyday Acts and Small Subversions</u> (Portland, Oregon: Eighth Mountain Press, 1994), 165.

A unique situation exists with the Naming Ceremony for a baby girl. Jewish tradition holds that a baby girl receives her name in the synagogue during the first Torah reading following her birth. Addressing this issue, Rabbi Joseph Telushkin, writes, "In recent years, with the rise of feminism, new ceremonies have been created to celebrate a girl's birth. Reform Judaism has developed a ritual for naming a girl called brit ha-hayim (covenant of life), and it is found in the Reform movement's home prayerbook, *Gates of the House*. Naming ceremonies for girls are performed by some Conservative and Modern Orthodox Jews as well. As of yet, there is no formal liturgy for this ritual, and copies of many different ceremonies are currently circulating."[15]

As Rabbi Telushkin suggests, more and more Jewish families are inventing a ritual that they see necessary. Because the Naming Ceremony for a girl has not been ritualized and formalized, it can lend itself to doubling as an Entrustment Ceremony. Families who design their own Naming Ceremony may consider incorporating elements of entrustment into that ritual. Among the two Entrustment Ceremonies that follow, the latter does just that. Either ceremony can be adapted to a number of adoptive situations, with birthparent(s) present, not present or represented by proxy.

For those families who wish to include birthparent(s), keep the following issues in mind:

— *Since both of these rituals are performed quickly after a child's birth (the Brit Milah when a boy is 8-days-old and the Simhat Bat shortly after a girl is born), inclusion of birthparent(s) should be at their discretion.*

— *Some birthparent(s) are grieving too heavily to participate in such a ceremony, while for others, taking part will facilitate the healing process. The rabbi and adoptive family should respect the individual grief response in birthparent(s). In such cases, an Entrustment Ceremony may always be scheduled later when it is more appropriate.*

— *On the other hand, some birthparent(s) are so committed to their decision of adoption and feel such a bond to the adoptive family that they are ready for immediate participation in an adoption ritual.*

---

15   Rabbi Joseph Telushkin, <u>Jewish Literacy: The Most Important Things to Know about the Jewish Religion, its People and its History.</u> (New York: William Morrow and Company, Inc., 1991), 610.

An Entrustment Ceremony

*(The following meaningful Entrustment/Transition
Ceremonies was written by Rabbi Norman Cohen of Bet
Shalom Synagogue in Hopkins, Minnesota. This ritual may
be lengthened or amended with inclusions from the chart
found on page 17. In this case, this rabbi prefers to use God
versus G-d as is traditional.)*

Rabbi: *The Talmud tells us, "Whoever brings up and adopts a child in his or her home, the
scripture ascribes it to them as though they had begot them."*

*Indeed, the greatest of all Jews in our history, Moses, was a child who was adopted into the
palace of the pharaoh. One of the greatest heroes of the holiday of Purim, Queen Esther, was
herself adopted by her uncle, Mordecai.*

*Of even greater theological significance is the fact that, in rabbinic literature, the metaphor of
adoption is used to describe our sacred relationship to God. God adopts King David,
legitimizing his dynasty and, beyond that, God adopts the people of Israel as God's own.*

In an open adoption where both birth and adoptive families are present:

*We here today are honored to share with two families the leaving and joining of this child
_____ from one family to another. We acknowledge the entrustment of the birthparent(s),
_____ who gave _____ the gift of life and have chosen the family of
_____ to be her/his adoptive family.*

In an adoption where birthparent(s) are not present, or are represented by proxy:

*We here today are honored to share in the joy of the joining of this child _____
with the _____ family, as they become one family, not only legally, but spiritually
before God. We also bless and acknowledge the entrustment of the birthparent(s) (NAME(S) IF
KNOWN) who gave _____ the gift of life. (Representing them are _____
and _____.)*

As you link yourselves together today, we ask that you recite the blessing which thanks God for giving us life and sustaining us.

Shehechiyanu — May every living creature thank you and praise You faithfully, our deliverance and our help. Praised are You, beneficent Lord to whom all praise is due.

And it is my privilege, as your rabbi, to ask for God's blessing upon you, now and always, in the words hallowed throughout our tradition...

The Priestly Benediction:
May the Lord bless you and keep you. May the Lord make His Glory shine upon you and be kindly toward you. May the Lord turn His Glory unto you and grant you peace. Numbers: 6:24-26

אֱלֹהֵי כָּל־חַי ׃

יְבָרֶכְךָ יְיָ וְיִשְׁמְרֶךָ ׃ יָאֵר יְיָ פָּנָיו אֵלֶיךָ וִיחֻנֶּךָּ ׃ יִשָּׂא יְיָ פָּנָיו אֵלֶיךָ וְיָשֵׂם לְךָ שָׁלוֹם ׃

Entrustment Ceremony
Welcoming into the Covenant
Naming Ceremony of a Baby Girl

(The following Naming Ceremony of a Baby Girl was designed to include the birthparent(s) in a combined ceremony of adoption transition and Welcoming into the Covenant.)

Rabbi: *Blessed be all who enter. May all of you who have come on this joyous occasion be blessed. This is the day which the Lord has made, let us be glad and rejoice on it.*

Water is a symbol of G-d sustaining us in our wanderings, sustaining us in our spiritual journeys as a people, and as individuals searching for meaning in our lives. Water is a symbol of the ultimate meaning of life and of the promise of salvation.

Today we mark the beginning of————Hebrew Name's———— journey as a member of the Jewish people, and we mark this journey's beginning with water.

*Here the birthparent(s) and adoptive parents could share the following symbolic act.

Your adoptive parents_____ and your birthparent(s) _____ will now wash your feet as a sign of our welcoming into the brit, the covenant between the Jewish people and G-d. Our prayer for you is that in all your future journeys through life, you will find guidance and sustenance in the traditions of the Jewish people.

Blessed are You, Adonai our G-d, Ruler of the Universe, Who is mindful of the covenant through the washing of the feet.

May this washing of your feet sustain you throughout your life.

*Readings from the Psalms may be shared at this point or participants may speak from their hearts.

If birthparent(s) are present:

We here today are honored to share with two families the leaving and joining of this child _____ from one family to another. We acknowledge the entrustment of the birthparent(s), _____ who gave _____ the gift of life and have chosen the family of _____ to be her/his adoptive family.

If birthparent(s) are not present or represented by proxy:

We here today are honored to share in the joy of the joining of this child _____ with the _____ family, as they become one family, not only legally, but spiritually before God. We also bless and acknowledge the entrustment of the birthparent(s)_____ who gave _____ the gift of life. (Representing them are _____ and _____.)

Rabbi: *And now formally we bestow upon this child the Hebrew name _____. May G-d who blessed our ancestors Abraham and Sarah, Isaac and Rebecca, Jacob with Leah and Rachel, bless the birthparent(s),_____ and the parents they have chosen _____ and their newborn daughter, _____.*

May _____ rear their daughter to adulthood imbued with love of Torah and the performance of good deeds, and may they be privileged to bring her to the wedding canopy.

Adoptive mother: *We give you the name_____in memory of ___[Name of One(s) Memorialized]_____. You have been entrusted to us by your birthparent(s),_____. They gave you the gift of life.**

Adoptive father: *We give you the Hebrew name _____ in memory of_____[Name of One(s) Memorialized]_____.*

This prayer could be said by adoptive parents together, by birthparent(s) or by both families.

We pray for the well being and good health of our daughter. Grant that she bring honor to the name she bears, and that she be a credit to this people. Bless her with a long life and good deeds.

All: *With what can we bless you but the riches of life:*
Eyes open wide to every flower and bird,
Ears attentive to both the great and the meek.
A smile of sunshine, feet to dance and hands to grasp.
A heart that dreams and a soul that sings!

Adoptive Parents Together:
May our daughter's life be one of
security and trust.
May our daughter's life shine with
dignity and freedom.
May our daughter's life know harmony
and the gift of peace.

Rabbi: *(to the adoptive parents) Once before at your wedding, you drank together from the cup of wine. Drink again with ___birth parent(s) name_____ in celebration of this life and in acknowledgement of the pain and the joy which unites these families around this child.*

All: *Baruch Atah Adonai, Elohaynu Melech Ha-Olam, Borei Pree HaGafen.*
Mazel Tov.

*In cases where birthparent(s) have given the middle name or helped name the child, it may be appropriate to mention at this point.

SUGGESTED READINGS AND SYMBOLIC ACTIONS

The following readings and actions are given to help in the design of a Jewish adoption ritual:

SUGGESTED READINGS AND BLESSINGS	SYMBOLIC ACTIONS
Psalm 121 Psalm 127 Psalm 128	Wrapping baby in either the birthfather or adoptive father's tallit (prayer shawl.)
Shehechiyanu	
HaMotzi	
"It is written (Judah b. Illai: Lamentations Rabbah 1:6:33)	
"See how precious children are: *The Shekhinah did not go with the* *Sanhedrin and priestly watches* *into exile, but it did go with the children."*	
"May the life of this child be one of happiness *and wisdom.* *Help us to lead our daughter/son in the footsteps of* *the great leaders of Israel, whose deeds continue to shine* *across the ages of our people.* *We praise You, G-d, whose Torah links the generations one to another."*	Blessings said for the child by birthparent(s) and adoptive parents, or said by proxy for birthparent(s).
"We praise You, who has created the fruit *of the vine."* (All present drink from wine cup.)	Birth and adoptive family drink wine or grape juice from the same cup.
(BOTH FAMILIES CAN RECITE TOGETHER) *"Blessed are you, Adonai, Ruler of the Universe,* *who has given us life, sustained us, and brought* *us to this moment."* *"Bless us, G-d - all of us together - with the light of Your countenance."*	A cup of wine and a loaf of hallah are presented. Families may break bread together.
"Praised are You, Adonai, Lord of the *universe, Creator of the fruit of the vine"* *"Praised are You, Adonai, Lord of the universe, Creator of the mystery of creation."* *"Praised are you, Adonai, Lord of the universe, Creator of everything for Your glory."*	Celebrant blesses the wine or grape juice.
"Praised are You, Adonai, Lord of the universe, who created human beings in *Your image and Your likeness, and out of their very selves You prepared for* *them a perpetual spiritual being. Praised are You, Lord, Creator of humanity."*	
"Praised are You, Adonai, Lord of the universe, who has such as these *Your creatures in Your world."* *"Praised are You, Adonai, Lord the universe, rememberer of the covenant* *and steadfastly faithful in Your covenant, keeping Your promise."* *"Praised are You, Adonai, Lord of the universe, who has sustained us in* *life and being and brought us to this very moment."*	

SUGGESTED READINGS AND SYMBOLIC ACTIONS

The following readings and actions are given to help in the design of a Jewish adoption ritual:

SUGGESTED READINGS AND BLESSINGS	SYMBOLIC ACTIONS
(FOR A GIRL) *"O sister! May you grow into thousands of myriads"* (Genesis 24:60) *May G-d make you as our mothers Sarah, Rebecca, Rachel and Leah.* *Adonai bless you and keep you.* *Adonai make His face to shine upon you and be gracious to you.* *Adonai lift up His face to you and grant you peace."*	
(FOR A BOY) *"O brother! May God make you as our fathers, Abraham, Isaac and Jacob.* *Adonai bless you and keep you.* *Adonai make His face to shine upon you and be gracious to you.* *Adonai lift up His face to you and grant you peace."*	
I Samuel 1:9-18 (Hannah's prayer)	The adoptive parent(s) present a gift or token to the birthparent(s).
Blessed are you, Adonai, Ruler of the universe who brings light into our life.	Birth and adoptive parent(s) light a candle together.

This blessing is recited over bread:

בָּרוּךְ אַתָּה יְיָ, אֱלֹהֵינוּ מֶלֶךְ הָעוֹלָם,
הַמּוֹצִיא לֶחֶם מִן הָאָרֶץ.

Before drinking wine: — :עַל יַיִן

בָּרוּךְ אַתָּה יְיָ, אֱלֹהֵינוּ מֶלֶךְ הָעוֹלָם, בּוֹרֵא
פְּרִי הַגָּפֶן.

CHRISTIAN ADOPTION RITUALS

Christian tradition provides many opportunities for using music, scripture and liturgy to create adoption rituals. Christian belief hinges on adoption as a theological tenet, humans being adopted by God through faith in Christ.

In a sense, all Christians are adopted persons.

Many scriptural passages lend themselves to adoption, including Ruth 1:16-17. Often repeated in weddings, Ruth's message to her mother-in-law has the sense of permanency, providing a "forever family" for the adopted child. For an older child who has been in multiple foster care settings, the reading and explanation of these verses can emphasize how those who are not blood relations can have a permanent bond.

As mentioned earlier, Hannah's Prayer, found in First Samuel 1:9-18, has application for both birthparent(s) and adoptive parents. The grief of infertility is presented as Hannah, "a woman of sorrowful spirit," speaks the bitterness she feels in her heart. That bitterness dissolves into a vow expressing the sacrifice that birthparents make in adoption; Hannah will give her child to the Lord. Eli's final blessing applies to both adoptive and birth families: "Go in peace, and the God of Israel grant thee thy petition that thou hast asked of him." The final verse presents the hope of peace and resolution for birthparents, "And she said, *Let thine handmaid find grace in thy sight.* So the woman went her way, and did eat, and her countenance was no more sad."

Although the focus in this book is on Entrustment Ceremonies, some churches have designed a <u>Baby Dedication</u> ritual that can be adapted to adoption. The Baby Dedication service is typically found in non-denominational and Charismatic churches which do not believe in baby baptisms or christenings.[16] The service commits the child to be raised to honor God, the parents taking that responsibility until the child is old enough to make his or her own decision regarding faith. The congregation is asked to pray for the parents and to be a part of this child's spiritual family.

Since non-denominational churches and Charismatic churches may forego traditional music and liturgy, the chart which follows the various denominations' services may not hold meaning for those who are designing a ritual. A Baby Dedication Service for an adopted child can still incorporate a prayer and blessing for birthparents who may

---

16   A Baby Dedication Service is also found in the Unitarian and Unitarian-Universalist Church.

or may not be present. Or it may entail the birthparent(s) handing the child to the adoptive parents and other meaningful inclusions.

Catholic tradition includes fixed sacraments which are set by the Universal Church and cannot be altered.[17] Still, there is room for sacramentals including the rosary and such services as The Thanksgiving for the Gift of a Child service (found in this book and in "Household Blessings and Prayers".) An Entrustment Ceremony could be incorporated around that service as well.

In the Protestant tradition, many churches consider baptism to be the most important of the seven sacraments; therefore, baptism is unalterable in any way. When one minister warns, "Be careful that you don't try to create a sacrament for adoption. The integrity of Christian sacraments must be preserved," he emphasizes the sanctity of religious ritual. In order to avoid such controversy, one constructing a ritual might incorporate aspects of *The New Zealand Prayer Book* instead.

In the Episcopal or Anglican tradition, *The New Zealand Prayer Book* emphasizes this idea in the preface to the Thanksgiving for The Gift of A Child service: "This service has no connection with Baptism, which is the sacrament of initiation in the Church, the body of Christ."

Thanksgiving for the Gift of a Child Services and Baby Dedications easily lend themselves to the incorporation of adoption. In some churches, not only is it ill-advised to combine adoption with baptism; it is not allowed. Always seek the guidance of your clergy in such matters.

The Book of Common Prayer of the Episcopal Church includes A Thanksgiving for the Birth or Adoption of a Child service which is included in both Spanish and English in this text. Notable in that service is the provision for an older child to "take" the man and woman as his or her parents.

In the pages which follow are examples of Christian Adoption Rituals from various churches.

---

17   In liturgical churches these sacraments include baptism, confirmation, the Eucharist, matrimony, orders, penance and extreme unction.

A Baby Dedication From The Assembly Of God
Dedication of Children[18]

Let some children's song be sung while the parents bring the child to the altar and the minister meets them there. Appropriate Scriptures can then be read, such as Mark 10:13-16; Matt. 19:13-15.

The pastor then addresses the congregation or assembled friends as follows:

"Dearly beloved, the family is a divine institution ordained of God from the beginning of time. Children are a heritage of the Lord committed by Him to their parents for care, protection, and training for His glory. It is meet[19] that all parents recognize this obligation and their responsibility to God in this matter. Jochebed of old trained her own child, Moses, after having given him to the Lord. Hannah recognized that her child was Jehovah's. The virgin Mary also brought the infant Jesus to the temple. The parents of this child likewise recognize the sacredness of their charge and now bring back to the Lord the treasure which He has intrusted to them. In so doing they recognize and hereby publicly acknowledge their responsibility for the nurture and admonition of this child in the ways of righteousness and godliness."

[*If birthparent(s) are present, they may receive the child and, in turn, present the child to the adoptive parent(s).]

---

18   Used by permission of R.M. Riggs <u>The Minister's Service Book.</u> (Springfield, Missouri: Gospel Publishing House, 1965), 43.

19   "It is meet" means "it is proper."

The minister shall then address the parents as follows:

"In the sight of God and in the presence of these witnesses, do you solemnly undertake to bring up this child in the fear and admonition of the Lord?"

They shall answer: *"We do."*

"Do you promise early to seek to lead him/her to accept Jesus Christ as Saviour and Lord?"

They shall answer: *"We do."*

"Do you promise as far as in you lies to set before him/her examples of godly and consistent lives?"

They shall answer: *"We do."*

Then, taking the child in his arms or laying hands upon its head, the pastor will say:

"In the name of the Lord Jesus, I dedicate this child, ———— , to God and His holy service."

The minister then offers the dedicatory prayer.

The congregation may sing another children's hymn in conclusion.

A Thanksgiving for the Birth or Adoption of a Child[20]

*As soon as convenient after the birth of a child, or after
receiving a child by adoption, the parents, with other
members of the family, should come to the church to be
welcomed by the congregation and to give thanks to
Almighty God. It is desirable that this take place at a
Sunday service. In the Eucharist it may follow the Prayer of
the People preceding the Offertory. At Morning or Evening
Prayer it may take place before the close of the Office.*

For an Adoption

The Celebrant addresses the congregation in these or similar words:
*Dear Friends: It has pleased God our heavenly Father to answer the earnest prayers of
_____ (and _____), member(s) of this Christian family, for the gift of a child. I bid
you join with them (and with _____ and _____) who now has a new brother
(sister) in offering heartfelt thanks for the joyful and solemn responsibility which is theirs by the
coming of _____ to be a member of their family. But first, our friends wish us, here
assembled, to witness the inauguration of this new relationship.*

The Celebrant asks the parent or parents
_____ (and_____), do you take this child for your own?

Parent(s) *I do.*

Then if the child is old enough to answer, the Celebrant asks _____, *do you take this
woman as your mother?*

Child. *I do.*

Celebrant *Do you take this man as your father?*

Child *I do.*

**Then the Celebrant, holding or taking the child by the hand, gives the child to the
mother or father, saying** *As God has made us his children by adoption and grace, may you
receive_____ as your own son (daughter).*

---

20 Used by permission of <u>The Book of Common Prayer.</u> (New York: The Church Hymnal Corporation and Seabury Press, 1977), 439.

CHRISTIAN ADOPTION RITUALS
(SPANISH)

Acción de Gracias por el Nacimiento o la Adopción de un Niño

Tan pronto como sea conveniente después del nacimiento de un niño, o de su adopción, los padres, junto con otros miembros de la familia, deben venir a la iglesia para que la congregación les dé la bienvenida, y para dar gracias a Dios todopoderoso. Es deseable que esto se efectúe en un servicio dominical. En la Eucaristía, puede seguir a la Oración de los Fieles, antes del Ofertorio. En la Oración Matutina o Vespertina, puede efectuarse antes del final del Oficio.

Si se prefiere, puede usarse una forma más breve de este rito, especialmente si se efectúa en el hospital o en el hogar; en tal caso, el Celebrante puede comenzar con el Acto de Acción de Gracias, o con la oración "Oh Dios, tú nos enseñaste". Puede leerse primero un pasaje de las Sagradas Escrituras. Los siguientes son apropiados: San Lucas 2:41-51, o San Lucas 18:15-17.
Durante las oraciones, los padres pueden expresar su gratitud con sus propias palabras.
En el momento apropiado, el Celebrante invita a los padres y a otros miembros de la familia a presentarse ante el Altar.

Por una Adopción

El Celebrante se dirige a nuestro congregación con éstas o otras palabras similares:
Mis amigos: Dios nuestro Padre celestial se ha dignado contestar las fervientes oraciones de _____ (y _____) miembros de esta familia cristiana, pidiendo el don de un hijo. Les invito a unirse a ellos (y a _____ (y _____), que ahora tiene un nuevo hermana) para ofrecer cordiales gracias por la gozosa y solemne responsabilidad que ahora tiene con la ilegada de _____ como miembro de su familia. Pero antes, nuestros amigos desean que nosotros, los aquí reunidos, seamos testigos de esta nueva relación.

El Celebrante pregunta a los padres:
_____ (y_____), *¿reciben a este niño como su propio hijo?*

Padre(s) *Sí, lo recibimos.*

Entonces, si el niño tiene la edad suficiente para contestar, el Celebrante le pregunta:
¿_____, recibes a _____ como tu madre?

Niño. *Sí, la recibo.*

Celebrante *¿Recibes a _____ como tu padre?*

Niño. *Sí, lo recibo.*

Then one or both parents say these or similar words *May God, the Father of all, bless our child _____ and us who have given to him/her our family name, that we may live together in love and affection; through Jesus Christ our Lord. Amen.*

HERE BIRTHPARENT(S), EITHER BY PROXY OR IN PERSON, MAY SAY THESE OR SIMILAR WORDS:

God, who understands and comforts the greatest loss, help me/us to love and let go. Grant me/us peace and bless this child as he/she joins his/her family.

Act of Thanksgiving

The Celebrant says *Since it has pleased God to bestow upon _____ (and _____) the gift of a child, let us now give thanks to him, and say together:*

The Song of Mary

My soul proclaims the greatness of the Lord,
my spirit rejoices in God my Savior;
for he has looked with favor on his lowly servant.
From this day all generations will call me blessed:
the Almighty has done great things for me, and holy is his Name.
He has mercy on those who fear him in every generation.
He has shown the strength of his arm,
he has scattered the proud in their conceit.
He has cast down the mighty from their thrones,
and has lifted up the lowly.
He has filled the hungry with good things,
and the rich he has sent away empty.
He has come to the help of his servant Israel,
for he has remembered his promise of mercy,
The promise he made to our fathers,
to Abraham and his children for ever.
Glory to the Father, and to the Son, and to the Holy Spirit:
as it was in the beginning, is now, and will be for ever.
Amen.

Luego el Celebrante, sosteniendo al niño o tomándolo de la mano, lo entrega a la madre o al padre, diciendo:

Así como Dios nos ha hecho sus hijos por adopción y gracia, reciban ustedes a _____ como su propio hijo.

En seguida, uno de los padres, o los dos juntos, dice éstas o otras palabras similares:

Que Dios, el Padre de todos, bendiga a nuestro hijo _____, y a nosotros que le hemos dado nuestro apellido, para que vivamos juntos en amor y afecto; por Jesucristo nuestro Señor. Amén.

Aqui, uno o dos padres de nacimiento, por poderes o en persona, dice éstas o otras palabras similares:

Que Dios, quien entiende y conforta las más grandes pérdidan, nos/me ayude a amor y dejar partir. Dame/nos paz y bendice a este/esta niño/niña que se une con su familia.

Acto de Acción de Gracias

El Celebrante dice:

Puesto que Dios se ha dignado conceder a _____ (y _____) el don de un nino, démosle gracias y digamos juntos:

Cantico de María

Proclama mi alma la grandeza del Señor,
se alegra mi espíritu en Dios mi Salvador,
porque ha mirado la humillación de su esclava.
Desde ahora me felicitarán todas las generaciones,
porque el Poderoso ha hecho obras grandes por mí;
su Nombre es santo.
Su misericordia llega a sus fieles, de generación en generación.
El hace proezas con su brazo: dispersa a los soberbios de corazón.
Derriba del trono a los poderosos, y enaltece a los humildes.
A los hambrientos los colma de bienes, y a los ricos despide vacíos.
Auxilia a Isreal su siervo, acordándose de la misericordia,
Como lo había prometido a nuestros padres,
en favor de Abrahán y su descendencia por siempre.
Gloria al Padre, y a Hijo y al Espíritu Santo:
como era en el principio, ahora y siempre,
por los siglos de los siglos.
Amén.

or this

Psalm 116

I love the Lord, because he has heard the voice of my supplication;
because he has inclined his ear to me whenever I called upon him.
Gracious is the Lord and righteous; our God is full of compassion.
How shall I repay the Lord for all the good things he has done for me?
I will lift up the cup of salvation and call upon the Name of the Lord,
I will fulfill my vows to the Lord in the presence of all his people,
In the courts of the Lord's house, in the midst of you, O Jerusalem.
Hallelujah!
Glory to the Father, and to the Son, and to the Holy Spirit:
as it was in the beginning, is now, and will be for ever. Amen.

or this:

Psalm 23

The Lord is my shepherd; I shall not be in want.
He wants me to lie down in green pastures and leads me beside still waters.
He revives my soul and guides me along right pathways for his Name's sake.
Though I walk through the valley of the shadow of death, I shall fear no evil:
for you are with me; your rod and your staff, they comfort me.
You spread a table before me in the presence of those who trouble me:
you have anointed my head with oil, and my cup is running over.
Surely your goodness and mercy shall follow me all the days of my life,
and I will dwell in the house of the Lord for ever.
Glory to the Father, and to the Son, and to the Holy Spirit:
as it was in the beginning, is now, and will be for ever. Amen.

The Celebrant then says this prayer

Let us pray.

O God, you have taught us through your blessed Son that whoever receives a little child in the name of Christ receives Christ himself: We give you thanks for the blessing you have bestowed upon this family in giving them a child. Confirm their joy by a lively sense of your presence with them, and give them calm strength and patient wisdom as they seek to bring this child to love all that is true and noble, just and pure, lovable and gracious, excellent and admirable, following the example of our Lord and Saviour, Jesus Christ. Amen.

o este:

Salmo 116

Amo al Señor, pues ha oído mi voz y mi súplica: porque ha inclinado a mí su oído,

siempre que le invoco. Clemente es el Señor y justo: sí, misericordioso es nuestro Dios.

¿Cómo pagaré al Señor por todos sus beneficios para conmigo?

Alzaré la copa de la salvación, y invocaré el Nombre del Señor.

Pagaré mis votos al Señor delante de todo su pueblo,

En los atrios de la casa del Señor, en medio de ti, oh Jerusalén.

¡Aleluya!

Gloria al Padre, y al Hijo y al Espíritu Santo:

como era en el principio, ahora y siempre,

por los siglos de los siglos. Amén.

o este:

Salmo 23

El Señor es mi pastor; nada me faltará.

En verdes pastos me hace yacer; me conduce hacia aguas tranquilas.

Aviva mi alma y me guía por sendas seguras por amor de su Nombre.

Aunque ande en valle de sombra de muerte, no temeré mal alguno;

porque tú estás conmigo; tu vara y tu cayado me infunden aliento.

Aderezarás mesa delante de mí en presencia de mis angustiadores;

unges mi cabeza con óleo; mi copa está rebosando.

Ciertamente el bien y la misericordia me seguirán

todos los días de mi vida, y en la casa del Señor moraré por largos días.

Gloria al Padre, y al Hijo y al Espíritu Santo:

como era en el principio, ahora y siempre, por los siglos de los siglos. Amén.

Entonces el Celebrante dice:

Oremos.

Oh Dios, tú nos enseñaste por tu bendito Hijo que cualquiera que reciba a un niño en el nombre de Cristo recibe a Cristo mismo: Te damos gracias por la bendición que has concedido a esta familia, dándole un hijo. Confirma su algría por medio de un sentido vivo de tu presencia entre ellos; dales serena fortaleza y paciente sabiduría, a medida que conducen a este niño a amar todo cuanto es verdadero y noble, justo y puro, amable y honorable, virtuoso y digno de elogio, siguiendo el ejemplo de nuestro Señor y Salvador Jesucristo. Amén.

CHRISTIAN ADOPTION RITUALS
(ENGLISH)

Prayers. The Celebrant may add one or more of the following prayers

For the BIRTHPARENT(S)

May God in his infinite mercy, provide comfort and solace for those who gave birth and made this noble decision of adoption for this child. May joy come from their sorrow, hope from their pain and strength from their adversity. Bless them as they release this child to his/her full potential. Just as Christ transformed water into wine, let their grief become the wine of liberation.

For the ADOPTIVE PARENTS —

Almighty God, giver of life and love, bless _____ and _____. Grant them wisdom and devotion in the ordering of their common life, that each may be to the other a strength in need, a counselor in perplexity, a comfort in sorrow, and a companion in joy. And so knit their wills together in your will and their spirits in your Spirit, that they may live together in love and peace all the days of their life; through Jesus Christ our Lord. Amen.

For a child not yet baptized

O eternal God, you have promised to be a father to a thousand generations of those who love and fear you: Bless this child and preserve his/her life; receive him/her and enable him/her to receive you, that through the Sacrament of Baptism he/she may become the child of God; through Jesus Christ our Lord. Amen.

For a child already baptized

Into your hands, O God, we place your child _____. Support him/her in his/her successes and in his/her failures, in his/her joys and in his/her sorrows. As he/she grows in age, may he/she grow in grace, and in the knowledge of his/her Savior Jesus Christ. Amen.

The celebrant may then bless both the adoptive family and birth family.

May God the Father, who by Baptism adopts us as his children, grant you grace. Amen.
May God the Son, who sanctified a home at Nazareth, fill you with love. Amen.
May God the Holy Spirit, who has made the Church one family, keep you in peace. Amen.

The Peace may be exchanged.

30

Plegarias El Celebrante puede añadir una o más de las siguientes oraciones:

Por los padres de nacimiento

Que Dios en su infinita bondad ofrezca soporte y consuelo a los que concibieron a este niño y tomaron la noble decision de darlo en adopción. Que su pena le convierta en alegria, su dolor en esperanza y su adersidad en fortaleza. Bendicelos por dejar partir a este niño hacia el desarrollo de su potencial. Asi como Cristo transformió el agua en vino, permite que su pena se transforme en liberación.

Por los adopción padres

Dios todopoderoso, dador de la vida y del amor, bendice a _____ y _____. Confiéreles sabiduría y devoción, para que ordenen su vida en común, de tal modo que cada uno sea para el otro fortaleza en la necesidad, consejero en la duda, consuelo en la tristeza y compañero en el gozo; y de tal modo entrelaza sus voluntades en tu voluntad, y sus espíritus en tu Espíritu, que vivan juntos en amor y paz todos los días de su vida; por Jesucristo nuestro Señor. Amén.

Por un niño aún no bautizado

Dios eterno, tú prometiste ser padre de mil generaciones de los que te aman y temen: Bendice a este niño y guarda su vida; recíbele y capacítale para recíbele, a fin de que, por el Sacramento del Bautismo, Ilegue a ser hijo de Dios; por Jesucristo nuestro Señor. Amén.

Por un niño ya bautizado

En tus manos, oh Dios, ponemos a tu hijo _____ Sosténlo en sus triunfos y en sus fracasos, en sus alegrías y en sus tristezas. Concede que, así como crece en edad, también crezca en gracia y en el conocimiento de su Salvador Jesucristo. Amén.

El celebrante puede entonces bendecir tanto a la familia adoptiva como a loa de nacimiento.

Dios Padre, que por el Bautismo nos adopta como hijos suyos, les conceda su gracia. Amén.
Dios Hijo, que santificó un hogar en Nazaret, les colme de amor. Amén.
Dios Espíritu Santo, que hizo a la Iglesia una familiar, les guarde en paz. Amén.

Puede intercambiarse la Paz.

Thanksgiving for a Newly Adopted Child[21]

On first holding a newly adopted child, on bringing the child into the home for the first time, and on other occasions before the child's baptism, this blessing may be given by the parents.

Birth And Adoptive Parents May Say This Together
God, our creator, cherish this child.
Jesus, our savior, protect him/her.
Holy Spirit, our comforter, strengthen him/her.

Or:

Source of all blessings, Protector of infants, look with favor on this child, _____.
Hold him/her gently in your hands. When he/she is reborn of water and the Holy Spirit, bring him/her into the Church, there to share in your kingdom and with us to bless your name for ever. We ask this through Christ our Lord.
Amen.

The parents (adoptive and birth, or birth represented by proxy) trace the sign of the cross on the child's forehead. *_____, may the Lord Jesus, who loved children, bless you and keep you in his love, now and forever.*
Amen.

Adoptive Parents' Thanksgiving:
O God, we give you thanks for _____, whom you have welcomed into our family. Bless this family. Confirm a lively sense of your presence with us, and grant us patience and wisdom, that our lives may show forth the love of Christ, as we bring _____ up to love all that is good.

Here the birthparent(s) might want to add their own blessing for the child.
We ask this through Christ our Lord.
Amen.

---

21   Catholic Household Blessings and Prayers (Washington D.C.: Bishops' Committee on the Liturgy, 1988), 234.

An Ecumenical Service of Adoption

Over 30 million Americans are participating in a movement of Protestant unity called "The New Communion." This ecumenical effort seeks to join Protestant denominations from various mainline churches.

The Consultation on Church Union, an ecumenical agency based in Princeton, New Jersey, has been designing liturgy and services towards the goal of Christian unity. The service, "An Order for Thanksgiving for the Adoption of a Child," strives to overcome differences between the denominations and to stress one unified ministry.

The churches that are participating (or who are still considering participating) in The New Communion include:

The African American Episcopal Church,
Christian Church (Disciples of Christ),
Episcopal Church,
Presbyterian Church in the United States,
United Methodist Church

African Methodist Episcopal Zion Church,
Christian Methodist Episcopal Church,
National Council of Community Churches,
United Church of Christ,
United Presbyterian Church
    in the United States of America.

An Order for Thanksgiving
for the Adoption of a Child[22]

The Order may begin with this presentation:

Members of Christ's family, I present to you —(Adoptive Parents)— and —(Name of child)— whose coming into their home they now acknowledge with gratitude and faith.

Then the minister says:

Within the family of Christ, the adoption of a child is an occasion for thanksgiving. Life is God's gift, and children are a heritage from the Lord. Therefore we who are entrusted with their care are given both great responsibility and opportunity.Because God has favored us through the coming of this child, let us offer our praise.

22   "An Order of Thanksgiving for the Birth or Adoption of a Child" is used by permission of The Commission on Worship, Consultation on Church Union 1980, 228 Alexander Street, Princeton, New Jersey 08540.

A hymn of praise, psalm or canticle may be sung.

For the adoption of a child, the following or another prayer is offered.
O God, you have adopted all of us as your children. We give thanks to you for the child who has come to bless this family and for the parents who have welcomed this child as their own. By the power of your Holy Spirit, fill their home with love, trust and understanding; through Jesus Christ our Lord. Amen.

The minister now asks:
What name have you given this child?

Those presenting the child respond.

However, if the name is to be conferred as a part of this Order, the minister instead asks:
What name do you now give this child?

Those presenting the child may place their hands upon the child. They respond,
We name you _____ .

If birthparents helped name the child, that could be indicated here.

If birthparent(s) are present, they may receive the child and, in turn, present the child to the adoptive parent(s). Appropriate words to that effect or vows between the families may be exchanged.

The minister then says to the (adoptive) family:
In accepting _____ as a gift from God, you also acknowledge your faith in Jesus Christ and the responsibility which God places upon you.

The members of the family respond saying or repeating after the minister:
We receive _____ from the hand of a loving Creator. With humility and hope we accept the obligation which is ours, to love and nurture (her/him) and to lead (her/him) to Christian faith by our teaching and example. We ask for the power of the Holy Spirit and the support of the Church that we may be good stewards of this gift of life.

The minister then says to the congregation:
The Church is the family of Christ, the community in which we grow in faith and commitment.

The congregation responds:
We rejoice to take _____ under our care. We seek God's grace to be a community in which the Gospel is truly proclaimed to all. We will support you and minister with you as workers together in Christ Jesus and heirs of his promise.

The minister takes the child and says:
_____ , may the eternal God bless you and watch over you. May Jesus Christ incorporate you into his death and resurrection (through baptism). May the Holy Spirit sanctify you and bring you to life everlasting.

The minister returns the child to the (adoptive) family.

At this time the name of the child may be entered into the Roll of Catechumens or similar record, if such is kept by the congregation.

The minister then offers this or another prayer.

Gracious God, from whom every family in heaven and on earth is named; Out of the treasures of your glory strengthen us through your Spirit. Help us joyfully to nurture _____ within your Church. Bring (her/him) by grace to baptism (to Christian maturity), that Christ may dwell in (her/his) heart through faith. Give power to _____ and to us, that with all your people we may grasp the breadth and length, the height and depth of Christ's love. Enable us to know this love, though it is beyond knowledge, and to be filled with your own fullness; through Jesus Christ our Lord. Amen.

The Lord's Prayer may be used here if not used elsewhere in service.

The minister may conclude the Order by saying:

Glory to God, who by the power at work among us is able to do far more than we can ask or imagine. Glory be given to this God from generation to generation in the Church and in Christ Jesus for ever! Amen.

New Zealand Designs a Far-Reaching Ritual for Adoption

In New Zealand half of the adult adopted persons know their birth origins.[23] This remarkable statistic comes after the passage of the Adult Adoption Information Act in 1985 which allows adult adoptees who are 20 to obtain their birth certificate.[24] Equal access is given to birthparents.

The Adult Adoption Information Act was accompanied by educational efforts regarding reunions and openness as well as a strong positive media campaign about the change in the law. Today most families in New Zealand now know of reunions among their relatives or community.[25]

New Zealand's shift in adoption practice accounts for the inclusion of birthparent(s) in the following Service, "Thanksgiving for the Gift of a Child." The copyright material is taken from *A New Zealand Prayer Book - He Karakia Mihinare o Aotearoa* (1989) and is used with permission. The Maori responses are included to emphasize the importance of cultural inclusion, particularly in adoptions of children whose cultural, ethnic and racial heritage differ from their adoptive parents.

---

23 Keith C. Griffith. <u>The Right To Know Who You Are</u>. (Ottawa, Ontario: Katherine C. Kimball, 1991), Section 15, 6.

24 In the United States there is no way of knowing how many adopted persons know their birth origin, but it certainly is not near the 50% range. Each state varies in its rules about opening adoption records, the rule tending to be more restrictive than lax. The older an adopted person, the less likely they are to search, probably because the culture of their adoption is so closed. Most adopted children today either know their birth origin or will be able to access it much more easily than their older peers.

25 Ibid., Section 15, 6.

Thanksgiving for the Gift of a Child

This service provides an opportunity for parents and families to give thanks for the birth or adoption of a child and to offer prayer for family life. It may take place in the home, the hospital, in church or some other suitable setting as soon as convenient after the adoption of a child.

This service has no connection with Baptism, which is the sacrament of initiation in the Church, the body of Christ.

A priest, deacon or duly authorised lay person may lead the service with the family.
Welcome

The minister greets the family and friends informally, and then says:
In the name of God, the giver of life, who creates and loves us all.

The minister continues in these or similar words.

English	**Maori**
Dear friends in Christ,	*E te whanau a te Karaiti*
we have come to celebrate the	
gift of this child, born into	
the world; given to us to love,	
to nurture and to enjoy.	

A hymn or song may be sung.

The minister may say to the parent(s):
_____ *and* _____ *, what name have you given this child?*

The family, holding the child, responds:
We have named you _____ .

The family may wish to explain the choice of name and may give a gift or token to the child. A Gospel may be presented with the words:
Receive this book.
In it is the good news of God's love.

The Ministry of the Word

One of the following or some other suitable psalm may be read:
Psalm 121, Psalm 127 or Psalm 128

One of the following or some other suitable scripture passage may follow:

1 Samuel 2:1-10   *Mark 10:13-16*

Luke 1:46-55   *Luke 2:21-32*

The minister may speak to those present.

A hymn or song may be included here.

The Thanksgiving

The parents of the child may say together:

God our Creator, thank you for the waiting and the joy,
thank you for new life and for parenthood,
thank you for the gift of _____,
entrusted to our care.
May we be patient and understanding,
ready to guide and forgive,
that in our love _____ may know your love.
May s/he learn to love your world
and the whole family of your children;
through Christ our life.
Amen.

Or the minister may pray

For the natural[26] parents of an adopted child:
God, whose nature is always to have mercy,
look down with love on _____ 's birth father and mother;
keep them in your good care, and give them peace in their hearts,
through Jesus Christ our Lord.
Amen.

The minister may add one or more of the following prayers:

God of the humble and hopeful, you bless those who believe when you promise.
Help us, like Mary and Elizabeth, simply to delight in the good things
you prepare for us, to say 'yes', and to trust that your strength and your love
will provide the wisdom needed by those who care for _____.
Amen.

We thank you God for this new person, child of your creation.
May the knowledge of you dawn on her/him,
may the love of you grow in her/him,
and may the grace of your Spirit draw her/him to you.
Amen.

---

26   In the United States "birth" is typically used and not "natural" parents.

The Family and Home

Eternal Spirit, Earth-maker, Pain-bearer, Life-giver,
Source of all that is and shall be, Father and Mother of us all,
Loving God, in whom is heaven, enfold this family with your grace.
May their home be a place of your presence, your forgiveness and your freedom.
May your will be done in them and through them this day and for ever.
Amen.

The minister concludes the prayers, saying one of the introductions to the Lord's Prayer.

Gathering our prayers and praises into one, let us pray as our Saviour teaches us

Or

As God's children and heirs with
Christ we cry in the Spirit, 'Abba!'

Our Father in heaven,
hallowed be your name,
your kingdom come,
your will be done,
on earth as in heaven.
Give us today our daily bread.
Forgive us our sins
as we forgive those who
sin against us.
Save us from the time of trial
and deliver us from evil.
For the kingdom, the power
and the glory are yours now
and for ever.
Amen.

Maori [27]

Kua akona nei tatou e to tatou Ariki,
ka inoi tatou

E to matou Matua i te rangi
Kia tapu tou Ingoa.
Kia tae mai tou rangatiratanga.
Kia meatia tau e pai ai
ki runga ki te whenua,
kia rite ano ki to te rangi.
Homai ki a matou aianei
he taro ma matou mo tenai ra.
Murua o matou hara,
Me matou hoki e muru nei
i o te hunga e hara ana ki a matou.
Aua hoki matou e kawea kia whakawaia;
Engari whakaorangia matou i te kino:
Nou hoki te rangatiratanga, te kaha, me te kororia,
Ake ake ake. Amine.

Final Prayer or Blessing

When a priest is present, the child and family are blessed, using either of these forms or another blessing.

The blessing of the God
of Sarah and of Abraham,
the blessing of the Son, born of Mary,
the blessing of the Spirit,
who broods over us as a
mother over her children,
be with you now and for ever.
Amen.

Ma te Atua koe e manaaki,
e tiaki i nga wa katoa,
e noho i roto i te aroha o te Atua;
ko te aroha hoki te mea nui.
Amine.

---

27   The child's language of origin can be used here in a translation of The Lord's Prayer.

The priest or minister concludes with this prayer:

Our Lord Jesus Christ be with you to defend you,
within you to keep you, before you to lead you,
beside you to guard you, and above you to bless you.
Amen.

The family responds:

All embracing God the hope of every generation,
complete our joy by your presence;
give us quiet strength and patient wisdom
as we nurture _____ in all that is good,
and true, and just, through Jesus Christ our
friend and brother. Amen.

Service for the Dedication of Children

by Reverend M. Susan Milnor[28]

The following service introduces a child to the congregation while celebrating the miracle of life. Adoption is specifically mentioned in order to show that forming a family through adoption is equally miraculous to forming a family through birth.

Three levels of dedication occur in this ceremony. The parents dedicate themselves to raising the child in a way that is healthy for him or her; and yet, which takes the rest of the world into ethical account. In the heart of the service, the child is dedicated "to the spirit of truth, justice and love" — in other words, to the deepest, most profound spirit in life. Finally, the members of the congregation dedicate themselves, as a community, to the child's spiritual nurturing.

Minister: *Today is a day of dedication, a day of welcome, a day of recognition. We welcome infants and children in love and hope.*

We welcome children born to their parents, who have witnessed the miracle of their entry into the world. We welcome children adopted by their parents who have participated in the miracle of loving choice.

(Here a rose, a symbol of life unfolding, is presented.)

Each is touched by a flower, a symbol of dedication. For whether a flower is beautiful or not; whether it comes into full bloom or not; whether it fulfills itself as a flower or not — depends on the nurture it receives. No flower grows alone, apart from the sunshine and rain, apart from the soil in which it lives. So, too, no child grows alone.

And so we come also recognizing the responsibility of parents, and of this religious community, to care. We recognize the precious unique worth of each person, symbolized in his or her name.

May this dedication be true and lasting. May it be ours.

---

28   The Universalist and Unitarian tradition includes a Child Dedication Ceremony which varies from church to church. This service was designed by Rev. M. Susan Milnor of the First Universalist Church in Minneapolis.

(To Parents) *We are born into this world as helpless infants, dependent for life and growth upon the love and wisdom of our parents, that we might be nourished in body, mind and spirit. Just so, every child should be received by loving arms and guided with understanding care.*

Upon you, the parents, rests the sacred joy of nurturing these young lives through the years between birth and maturity. May you be guided by loving memories, worthy aspiration and a joyful heart. May your sense of responsibility be equal to the promise that is theirs.

Will the family come forward, please.

Do you promise that to the best of your ability you will nurture and instruct this child in the way of good living for him/her and for humankind?

Parents: *We/I do.*

Minister: *(NAME OF CHILD:)* _____, *with the touch of this rose, symbol of a beautiful life and unfolding, I dedicate you to the service of truth, justice and love. May the Spirit of Life be with you always.*

(The minister takes the child, lifts or leads him/her before the congregation and pronounces his/her name.)

Minister or the Director of Religious Education: *(To Congregation)*
Members and friends of this church, will you receive these children now into your loving care? Will you provide for their questing spirits, and will you grow with them? If so, please answer "We will."

Congregation: *We will.*

Minister: *Would you read responsively with me the litany of dedication and welcome.*

Litany of Dedication
We dedicate these children to the highest and the best in life, to the freedom and discipline of this community, to the great quest for mystery that lies in their own hearts.

Congregation: *We dedicate ourselves to making this church a place of spiritual growth for children. We dedicate ourselves to making the world a place fit for children.*

Minister: *We embark now on that journey together.*

All in unison: *Children, we welcome you into this world and into this community. In your names may all of us find joy. By your worth may generations to come be blessed.*

Minister: *(Prayer)*
Oh Spirit of life, For the gift of childhood, the innocence and laughter which keep the world young, we lift up thankful hearts. May these children whom we have dedicated today receive abundantly the blessings of love, health, knowledge and wisdom. May they in turn render them back richly into our common heritage. Remembering that those who follow must inherit their world from us, we dedicate ourselves to our part in building a more just and whole human order.
May it be so.

Service for Giving
a Child in Love

The following service is appropriate for Jewish or Christian families. The prayers were contributed by the Seton Center in St. Paul, Minnesota, Rabbi Michael Gold and Rabbi Jack Reimer. The service includes both birthparent(s) and adoptive parent(s) and can be adapted to their presence or absence.

by Maureen Connelly[29]

Song of your choice: *To be played on cassette, sung, or played on guitar or other instrument.*

Prayer: *Great Creator - you who form us in your image, we thank you for your compassion and understanding in times of sadness and letting go. In the midst of our pains and joys, we gather today to give you thanks for this gift of new life. We thank you for this child's birthparent, who brought her/him into this world. At this time of letting go, we thank you for your presence which bonds us together in love.*

Reflection: *by Chaplain or Clergy*

Reflection: *by Birthmother if she so desires.*
(She does not have to do anything here. However, if she wants, she can read her letter to her baby, read a poem, do what she desires.)

Blessing of the Child *(Chaplain/Clergy holding the baby.)*
Lord God, you who are mother and father to us, send forth your abundant blessing on this child who is made in your image. We pray this child will have the best home possible, one filled with faith, hope and deep love. A home and parents who will love as much as this child has been loved. Watch over and protect this child forever and ever.

Chaplain/Clergy speaks a blessing from the Birthparent(s).
Dear God,
I look to you at this turning point of my life,
as I place my beloved child for adoption.
You, who knows the hearts of all creatures, know the pain I feel.
Give me strength and courage, the strength to love and let go,
the courage to live through the moments of doubt and sadness,

29   Maureen Connelly. <u>Given in Love.</u> (Omaha, Nebraska: Centering Corporation, 1990).

knowing I made the best choice I could.
God, bless my child.
Help this child grow up healthy and happy.
Guide this child in this life to know Your ways.
Help this child to know that out there
is always someone who loves him/her.
Finally, You, the master of all life,
help us realize that none of us own our children.
Some are given the privilege of conceiving a child.
Some are given the privilege of raising a child.
Thank you for granting me the privilege of giving birth to this child.
May I always be worthy of your love and your blessing.

Prayer for Adopting Parents from the Birthparents *(Everyone)*

Bless the parents who will raise this child.
Give them wisdom in their parenting.
Help them love and protect this child.
Even if we never meet, we share so much.
We are partners in the creation of a human being.
We thank you for their compassion and their caring.
Give them strength and patience,
gentleness and humor.
We know they are excited now. We know they are
as delighted as any expectant parents in the world.
Soon they will have a day they will never forget,
when this beautiful child comes home to them.
Be with them as they guide and direct.
Be present during sickness and anxiety.
Be there, Lord, when they need you.
We are privileged to be part of their love, God.
We are honored to give this most precious of all gifts.
Bless this couple and this family, Dear God.

Closing Response: *We Remember Them*

Chaplain/Clergy with Response from People

In the rising of the sun and its going down, we remember them.
In the blowing wind and the chill of winter, we remember them.
In the opening of buds and in the rebirth of Spring, we remember them.
In the blue sky and warmth of Summer, we remember them.
In the rustling of leaves and the beauty of Autumn, we remember them.
In the beginning of the year and when it ends, we remember them.
When we are weary and in need of strength, we remember them.
When we are lost and sick at heart, we remember them.
When we have joys we yearn to share, we remember them.
So long as we live, they too shall live,
for they are now part of us, as we remember them.

Final blessing by Chaplain/Clergy

CHRISTIAN ADOPTION RITUALS

The following chart has Biblical, musical and symbolic suggestions that can be used in designing an appropriate ritual. The musical selections can be found in many hymnals.

SUGGESTED READINGS, MUSIC AND SYMBOLIC ACTIONS

Biblical Readings and stories	Music	Symbolic Actions
David and Saul Eli and Samuel	"Once in Royal David's City"	Light candles.
Christ's Dedication in the Temple Ruth and Naomi	"St. Elisabeth/ Father of Mercy, Lover of All All Children."	Wrap child in piece of new clothing to represent new life.
Christ with Anna and Simon (The significance is that Christ is ordained by God and put the dedication of His relationship in the context of faith.) Psalm 121 Psalm 127 Psalm 128	"Savior, Like a Shepherd lead us." "All Things Bright and Beautiful" "Behold a Little Child: Arthur's Seat"	
1 Samuel 1: 9-11, 20-28, 2:26 (birth & presentation of Samuel)		
1 Samuel 1:9-18 (Hannah's prayer)		Presentation of gifts between birth and adoptive parent(s).
Mark 3:35 "For whosoever shall do the will of God, the same is my brother, my sister, and mother."	"All People that on Earth do Dwell"	
Mark 10:13-16, Mark 19:13-15 or Luke 18:15-17 (Jesus blesses the children.)	"Joyful, Joyful We Adore Thee." "Love Divine"	Display a coat of arms or quilt created by birth and adoptive family.
Luke 1:46-55 Mary's Magnificat	"Magnificat"	Designate music to honor birthparents.
Luke 2:21-32 Jesus presented at the Temple in Jerusalem. Matthew 12:46-50 (Christ speaks of his new relationships.)		Read "The Sacrifice Flower" page 67.
Luke 8:19-21 repeats the story of the Beatitudes.		
Luke 2:41-51 or Luke 18:15-17		

SUGGESTED READINGS, MUSIC AND SYMBOLIC ACTIONS

Biblical Readings and stories	Music	Symbolic Actions
1 John 4:7-10 (little children are assured.)	"Cradle Hymn" (lyrics by Isaac Watts, melody by Harmonia Sacra)	Family members form circle around child
	"God be With You"	Pay tribute to absent birthparents.
	"We Gather Together" **Anthems:** "Let All the World in Every Corner Sing." John Rutter's "For the Beauty of the Earth" "Hail Thee, Festival Day."	Blessing of the families.
	Hymns of dedication and reconciliation: "Take My Life and Let It Be" "Jesu, Jesu, Fill Us with Your Love" *Congregation can sing as a round.*	
	Canticle Song of Zechariah	
	Spirituals "He's Got the Whole World in His Hands" "Over My Head I Hear Music in the Air" "Swing Low, Sweet Chariot"	

SECULAR ADOPTION RITUALS

*"That which is not celebrated, that which is not ritualized,
goes unnoticed, and in the long run those feelings and
happenings will be devalued. The smallest events can be
made into great moments of our lives by taking the time to
celebrate them."* [30]

Zsuzsanna Budapest

Secular is defined as pertaining to the world or to things not spiritual or sacred. Although a handy label, "secular" is rarely accurate because it places people outside the bounds of a belief system. Not all things spiritual and sacred are found inside of religion, and people may define spirituality as seeking or believing in something larger than oneself. Few readers will find themselves fitting within the dictionary definition of "secular."

Despite the difficulty with semantics, secular rituals are a part of a new paradigm that allows ritualists to reflect their creativity and inner nature. Some rituals are beginning to reflect a shift away from prescribed actions, symbols and doctrines, focusing more upon what participants can bring to and take away from the ritual. For instance, a wedding may have guests state their hopes for the couple. A funeral can be designed around the one who is remembered, perhaps offering friends playing in a jazz band or a memorial corner created around the deceased person's travels. A welcoming ritual for a baby may have each guest contribute a patch for a community-made quilt.

Those who design adoption rituals outside of religious parameters may have very personal reasons for doing so. In cases of open adoptions where birth and adoptive families are of different faiths, a secular ritual can unify families without offending either. Others may not belong to an organized religion and may not be comfortable in a religious setting.

Joseph Campbell once attributed spirituality to the practice of rituals, saying, "A ritual can be defined as an enactment of a myth. By participating in a ritual, you are actually experiencing a mythological life. And it's out of that participation that one can learn to live spiritually."[31] Campbell suggests that by performing a ritual, one begins to distill and define his/her beliefs. The ritual becomes an initiation ceremony, granting the participant membership into a new definition of himself or herself.

It is vitally important that the ritual be meaningful within the context of the various

---

30   Vivienne Margolis, <u>Fanfare for a Feather</u> (San Jose, California: Resource Publications, Inc., 1991), Preface
31   Joseph Campbell, <u>The Power of Myth</u> (New York: Doubleday 1988) 182.

participants' beliefs. The material that follows can be adapted to religious rituals or it may stand by itself in a "non-religious" context.

Designing a Ritual Carries its own Meaning
"Being Familied"

Because rituals are both physical and symbolic, they provide understanding and affirmation of the event of adoption. An adoption ritual increases understanding by paying attention to the child's history as well as his/her present position within the adoptive family. That duality is not the core of the child's being, but it - like any major circumstance in the child's life - becomes a part of his or her identity. The ritual affirms adoption as a unique way to form a family without blood ties. In the pages ahead are ideas on how to blend many elements that can contribute to an adoption ritual.

To design an adoption ritual, begin by picking and choosing what the participants need, adding personal touches that are meaningful. There are no bounds to the planners' creativity or to the materials, people and symbols that can be included. Look around and decide which colors, setting, flowers and seasons best fit the intent of the ritual. Then, just sit down and do it.

Penny Needham has facilitated adoption support groups for many years in the middle school where she teaches. She says, "I happen to think that the process of designing the ritual is as important as going through the ritual. One of my students in an adoption group was older when he was adopted; in fact he had experienced many placements. He told the judge he wanted to call his adoption, 'being familied.'"

Designing a "being familied" ritual for an older child will include different elements than for a baby. For the older child, inclusions may be based on the child's background and history, and should be stated in words that are understandable to the child. In one case a 10-year-old child was told, "You were once a library book on loan to family after family. By taking your family's name, you now belong to them. No one else can ever check you out and take you home on loan." The analogy was clear to the child and may be useful for others who are creating rituals.

A "Crossing-Over Ritual" may also be used to express the transition of an older child into an adoptive family. Using a real bridge or a facsimile, each participant can walk over an "adoption bridge." The beginning point symbolizes where they have been. The bridge can cross over troubled waters, just as in the Simon and Garfunkle song. Loving hands can guide the child safely across this bridge where the adoptive family will greet and embrace him/her.[32]

---

32   A Crossing-Over Ritual is described in Gay and David Williamson's <u>Transformative Rituals</u> (Deerfield Beach, Florida: Health Communications, Inc., 1994), 105.

Both older and younger children enjoy celebrations, so an adoption ritual should include singing and light-hearted activities. Readings and long speeches should be kept to a minimum. For an international adoption of a child, aged 4 to 8, Ann Turner's *Through Moon and Stars and Night Skies* would be appropriate. Dr. Seuss's *Oh, The Places You'll Go* or *On the Day You were Born* fit a child 5 to 10.

In transracial adoptions, paying homage to the child's culture should be an integral part of the ritual. The child's heritage can be represented by:

— *culturally specific music*

— *potpourri of herbs*

— *clothing*

— *flowers native to the child's country*

— *aromas*

— *language*

— *food*

— *objects*

Following the ritual, the sharing of food is traditional among many cultures. Here is another opportunity for family and guests to celebrate the ethnicity of the child.

As Penny Needham suggests, designing a ritual may be as important as performing the ritual. Although we may be uncomfortable actually inventing or altering tradition, doing so will allow the uniqueness of our child to be more fully expressed than a traditional ritual might allow.

Define the purpose of the ritual and why it should be performed. Think of "intent" or the goal of the ritual. Seeing the ritual as a simultaneous journey and destination may help travellers plot the trip.

As the planning process begins, consider what the child needs to have said, done, or included with his/her passage into adoption. It may help to imagine the child as a teenager or an adult viewing and hearing about this ritual. Even if the child is an infant, the ritual will serve as a historical marker, if recorded on video, film or in writing. Gifts and vows may be exchanged, a guest book signed and stories about that day passed down.

The second factor in ritual design must be the birthparents. Each adoption is unique and requires attention and sensitivity to the birthparent's individual situation. There are many factors to consider regarding inclusion of birthparents in the ritual. They may live 10,000 miles away or three blocks down the street. Their identity may be confined to a few sentences written on paper work, or it may involve videotapes and a detailed genealogy. They may have written a letter to the child that is in safe-keeping with the adoptive parents, signed only with their first name(s). Or, in an open adoption, they may attend and participate in the ritual.

In an open adoption, the birthparent(s)' emotions in the early stages of the adoption may affect their participation in a ritual. They may prefer to have a separate ritual that marks their relinquishment and their changing roles in the child's life.[33] Perhaps at a later time, they may decide to participate with the adoptive family in an entrustment ritual. In open adoptions, rituals should always be adapted to birthparent(s)' circumstances.

To exclude birthparents physically or symbolically from the adoption ritual will fragment and diminish meaning for everyone. Adoptive parents who acknowledge birthparents find their sense of parental entitlement to that child is strengthened rather than eroded.[34] Certainly, in years to come, the child will have a better appreciation of his/her adoption if his/her family of origin was integrated into the ritual through actual participation, by proxy or in other ways.

In open adoptions, exchanging vows and promises between birth and adoptive parents is beneficial. Sandy Sperrazza, a birthmother and active member of Concerned United Birthparents (C.U.B.) advises, "It is important to exchange promises or vows. It isn't just birth family to adoptive family. Adoptive families have to give some vows and promises back to the birth family. They could join in some kind of philosophy or prayer together."

The third consideration in the ritual is the adoptive family. Their part in the ritual is to welcome the child into their family, to express their blessing and gratitude to the birthparents, to vow to care for the child and to incorporate the child into the family.

Welcoming a child can be accomplished by the child being handed by the birthparents or the celebrant to the adoptive family. Holding the child while a lullaby is sung or played is a welcoming gesture. A welcome can be printed on an invitation to the ritual or on a program handed out to guests. Banners, balloons, gift-exchanges or flowers can also be welcoming tributes.

Expressing gratitude to and a blessing for birthparents is best done by speaking sincerely. Those who are not public speakers may feel more comfortable having someone else read their written words.

Adoptive parents can recite vows in a call and response manner, or they may design their own vows to be spoken. If there are other children in the family, they will need to be assigned a part in the ritual, perhaps vowing to be a loving sister or brother.

Naming a child declares and defines family membership. Other ways to signify the child's place in the family are through readings or songs that express thoughts about family life, or lighting a candle to show family unity.

Finally, there are the guests. Extended family members of both birth and adoptive families and special friends may also make vows regarding the child. Significant guests serve as witnesses to the ritual and as a larger community who will watch and help nurture the child.

---

33 Maureen Connelly's Service for a Child Given in Love works well for this purpose. See pages 43-44.
34 Lois Ruskai Melina and Sharon Kaplan Roszia. The Open Adoption Experience. (New York: Harper Collins, 1993), 133.

Among the guests, adults who act in the role of godparents may speak for the child, vowing for them "I receive you as my parents." In time the child may speak for himself/herself in annual rituals that may be repeated as an Adoption Arrival Day or Entrustment Ceremony Day.

Who leads?

Rituals typically have a celebrant, facilitator or guide. In cases of open adoption, this person can be someone chosen by the birth and adoptive families acting together. Perhaps it will be someone who was instrumental in the adoption or someone chosen from outside the process. A facilitator can be an adoption worker, a therapist or counselor, friend to either family, or a judge or person with standing in the community.

Sally Watson, an Adoption Advisor, was chosen to facilitate an Entrustment Ceremony that took place in a public rose garden in Benicia, California. She describes that ritual, saying, "Since 'Rose' was a part of the baby's name, this was as appropriate as the beautiful rose bush planted in her honor that day by the couple who had introduced the birthparents to the adopting parents. A picnic was laid out and then we all gathered in a kind of horseshoe-shaped arrangement with the baby in her tiny carrier at the open end. The adopting parents were on one side, facing the birthparents on the other side with the baby between them. The adopting parents made a touching statement to the birthparents, and going around the circle, everyone said something if they wanted to, or made a silent wish for the baby and all the parents. The birthparents made a touching statement to the adopting parents, and then the birthfather reached down to a tape-player and out came the strains of 'The Rose'. Even the facilitator is allowed a few tears at an Entrustment, and believe me, I shed mine along with everyone else that day." [35]

Watson has the qualities needed in a facilitator: the caring attention to everyone's needs and an understanding of what those needs might be. As families plan their adoption ritual, they can seek such a person to direct the ritual.

---

35   Used by permission from Pact Press, Spring of 1993 issue, Volume 2, Number 1, 3315 Sacramento Street, Suite 239, San Francisco, California 94118.

Choosing a Setting

Entrustment and Welcoming Ceremonies may be held in a variety of places. Appropriate settings include a hospital room, a judge's chambers, a park, beside a lake or the ocean, or a private home.

Whatever the setting, it should be significant to the ritual. One adoptive mom said, "We held our Entrustment Ceremony on a boat over water because we wanted not to be on someone's property. We didn't want to be caught up in ownership which is not at all what adoption is about. The water symbolized birth and life. The lake belonged to everyone."

"In our garden are many perennials," said an adoptive father. "We based our ritual on that cycle of life and the permanence of our commitment. In that garden are two plum trees, both needed in cross-pollination to bear fruit. We wrote a ceremony that included that reference to our family and our son's birth family, he being the child of two families."

A rose garden near a park became the setting of another entrustment ceremony. The red roses in full bloom were used to demonstrate love for the child, while the budding yellow roses were the symbol of the growing friendship between the birth and adoptive parents.

A peace garden, although Japanese, became the spot for a Welcoming Ceremony for a baby adopted from Korea. Plants native to Korea were tossed into a pond as a tribute to the missing birthparents.

In cases of open adoption, rituals may be held in either a birthparent's home or an adoptive parent's home. Sandy Sperrazza, a birthmother, gave the following reason for her preference for having the ritual in the adoptive parent's home: "For the adoptive parents to be willing to share their home for the ritual and not just go to a public space is a very strong statement. It lets the birthparents see where that child will be raised, will eat breakfast, will sleep. That in itself is a gift and not an invasion of privacy or security."

Holding a ritual in a birthparent's home may also provide balance between birth and adoptive family members. There, extended birth family members may have more freedom to participate and say goodbye to the child.

Many cultures not only pay attention to selecting a place for the ceremony, but also preparing the place for the ceremony. Whatever setting is chosen, the first part of the ritual may include purifying or purging the space of non-ceremonial elements.

This step entails setting aside the environment for the specific purpose of holding a ritual. Native Americans do this by burning sage. Westerners burn incense or candles. Japanese toss salt into the ring before a Sumo match that is as much ritualistic as it is sport.

Author, Diane Stein, suggests that after the purification, the ritual begin by "casting the circle." [36] Casting the circle transforms a space into a setting that is appropriate for a ritual. She says that by as simple an act as lighting a candle and acknowledging the people who are present, a living room is transmuted beyond its physical dimensions. Arrangement of participants into a horseshoe or a circle and background music may also serve this purpose, according to Stein.

Ritualist, Janis Dehler, suggests other ways to prepare the place for a ritual may include having participants pass a candle or breathe deeply and say their names individually. [37] For outdoor rituals, she confines and defines the space by acknowledging each of the four directions. She may have those present form an outer circle that designates north as the earth and thus the body, east as the air and mind, south as fire and spirit, while west represents water and emotions. Otherwise the outdoors may seem too large and overwhelming to accommodate the ritual.

Gifts

Gifts are integral parts of rituals. In birth rituals, gifts typically represent a legacy and hopes for the future.

In an adoption ritual, gifts can have these purposes:

— *symbolizing the journey made by the child as he/she joins the new family,*

— *marking the country and/or family of origin as the beginning of the journey,*

— *marking the adoption itself, the destination of the journey.*

Gifts Marking the Adoption Journey:
Moving a Child Geographically and Emotionally

All children make a journey to their adoptive family, whether they fly across an ocean, go directly from the hospital to their family or move through the foster care system. The journey to adoption will be the most significant trip of a child's life. As such, it needs to be marked and acknowledged through gifts.

36   Diane Stein. Casting the Circle: A Women's Book of Ritual. (Freedom, California: Crossing Press, 1990) 49-50.
37   Janis Dehler, interview by author.

For children who travel from other countries, the end of the journey is often described and documented, but the journey itself is seldom marked. A baby or small child who is accompanied by an escort from Korea, South America, the Philippines or India will have no memory of their momentous journey.

The agency or the adoptive family can arrange for the escort to bring a small gift that symbolizes the trip. Most airlines offer pilot wings to small children, and models of the airplane are usually available. A photo taken on the airplane of the escort holding the child will hold great meaning. With some effort on the part of those responsible for arranging the travel, the child's passage can later be "recalled."

An adoption journey that passes through foster care can include written descriptions by the foster care providers of that child's daily life. Feedings, events and behaviors can be recorded. The people who served as interim family to the child can be photographed. Even for an older child who will remember his/her time in foster care, the physical record of those days, months or years needs to be retained.

Holly van Gulden, author of *Real Parents, Real Children: Parenting the Adopted Child,* is horrified by how casually children are passed through the foster care system. During the moves, children may watch clothing and cherished possessions placed into garbage bags instead of boxes. The goal appears to get the child and their belongings transferred in the most expedient manner.

She suggests that perhaps unrealized, humans ritualize their transitions. Items are boxed and labeled, and discussions take place around where each article will go in the new house or apartment. A moving van arrives with a crew of workers who bustle about the work of moving, or friends and family volunteer their services. A goodbye is felt, if not stated, to the house and rooms and yard.

Van Gulden believes that for foster children, at the very least a suitcase or a box needs to be packed to mark each significant transition. Children need a chance to say more than a hurried goodbye. Even more, children need "gifts" to follow them. A toy the child played with while in the home, a photo album of the family interacting with the child, or books read at night before bedtime can all be appropriate gifts.

Domestic adoptions of infants and small children typically include a bequeath from birthparents. Gifts can include the infant picture taken in the hospital, footprints, the medical bracelet or any other token of birth. Birthparent(s) often choose to give articles of significance such as a baby blanket, a stuffed toy or sleeper. Such gifts can always be made an integral part of a ritual.

Gifts Marking the
Country and/or Family of Origin

Gifts that mark a pre-adoptive time are invaluable to persons who are adopted. Such gifts fill in gaps in the child's history and also say that someone cared enough to give a token or to record time spent with the child.

One adult, adopted at the age of three, said, "Look at my family albums and you'd think I was never born. All the photographs of me were taken when I was three or older. I can't remember anything that took place before my adoption."

A teen, who travelled to Korea and located the orphanage where she had lived, said, "I was thrilled to find a worker who remembered me and told me a few stories about my time there. I recorded her words which mean more to me than I can say."

Another adult, who was adopted as a child, recalls, "My birthmother was not allowed to give me her high school ring. She was 18-years-old, and it was her most prized possession, but the adoption agency and maternity home refused her wish. Later she gave me the ring when we met." She treasures the ring that is a traditional symbol of the circle of life, both unbroken and unending.

Families who travel long distances to meet their child in his or her native country can collect various articles from that country in advance of a ritual. Photo albums based on the setting and the people who were a part of the child's pre-adoptive life can be created. Orphanage workers, foster care providers, other children and even pets will be invaluable mementoes in the future.

Gifts that
Mark the Adoption

Giving gifts that mark the adoption serve the purpose of calling attention to the "dual citizenship" of adopted persons. Birthparents may give a gift that signifies the family of origin, or a gift may be extended on their behalf. The adoptive family may then present their gift, and in some cases, a collaborative gift may be given to represent both families.

Sandy Sperrazza suggests that birthparents who are actively involved in the adoption complete a family history to be presented at the ritual. She says, "The child's history is really with the birth family on some level. The gift could be a history book with pictures and stories of Grandpa. It could be a family heirloom like a family Bible. That gift of ancestry would be received formally, marking that transition, and given to the adoptive parents on behalf of that child."

Providing birth family history, through a picture album or a genealogy, assists the child in his/her future exploration of identity issues. For many adopted children who have no pictures of their pre-adoptive life and no marking of the joining to their adoptive family, the albums will be immensely valuable.[38]

Even for a child who has very little information about his/her pre-adoptive history, a lifebook can be created. According to Vera Fahlberg, author of *A Child's Journey Through Placement,* a lifebook "is an account of the child's life conveyed by words, pictures, photographs and documents."[39] The adoptive parents can work with a child to fill in the missing pieces, gathering and arranging materials that organize the early part of the child's life in chronological order.

The gift from the adoptive family may include their record of waiting for the child's arrival. In international adoptions, a scrapbook may be created that includes pre-adoptive photographs of the child that were sent from the country of origin, paperwork or even a journal written by the waiting adoptive family. Any item that includes the child's name done in calligraphy, needlepoint or engraving will be a keepsake of the adoption. A letter that describes in detail "the day you joined our family" makes a wonderful gift, as does a videotape of the day's events.

Some gifts can be a collective effort, created jointly by adoptive and birth families to mark the adoption. Quilts can have contributions from various family members, each patch containing a special wish or symbol for the child. Just as native Americans weave designs into a blanket to give it meaning and magical properties, a gift that incorporates both birth and adoptive families can carry its own magic, expressing the love and unity of two families who cared about the child's future.

---

38 One resource developed by Centering Corporation is <u>With Courage and Love: A Birthmother's Journal.</u> (See Helpful Resources Section for more information.)

39 Vera I. Fahlberg, M.D. <u>A Child's Journey Through Placement</u> (Indianapolis, Indiana: Perspective Press, 1991), 368.

A shadow box presents the opportunity to create a composite of gifts. Booties and a rattle that came from the birthparents can be placed beside booties and a rattle that were contributed by the adoptive parents. These or other articles could be glassed and framed inside a shadow box that is displayed within the child's home.

Content:
Symbolic and Literal

A symbol is not mere poetic fancy; it is the clothing of a spiritual reality in a conceptual garment so that its nature may be more readily perceived by our literal minds and thus we can see our way to choosing. [40]

A *symbol is not mere poetic fancy,* says author, Gail Godwin, trying to help the reader get beyond a natural prejudice against symbolism. Most of us have raised our hands in an English class to offer what turned out to be the "wrong" interpretation of a symbol in a novel or short story. Such incidents conveyed the faulty message that symbols are author's fancy tricks that can only be interpreted by teachers. No wonder we fail to recognize the symbols around us and balk at seeking meaningful symbols that help us "see our way to choosing."

Adoption rituals need to contain symbols that help participants choose the personal meaning of adoption within their lives. Suggestions of how to use objects symbolically are given in the pages to follow.

Perhaps the most dynamic symbol that identifies humans is a name. Some names are literal, the parents choosing that name because they like the sound of it. An American child often has a trendy name that, like other fads, fades in popularity as the child becomes older. Then the name may see a revival in popularity.

Many cultures recognize that names provide far more than identity. Depending on the culture, a name may indicate genealogy, one's place in a family, physical or character attributes and many other important traits. More importantly, names define us or as author Alex Haley wrote, let us know who we are.

Haley created a powerful scene in *Roots*[41] in which Kunte Kente lifts his daughter to the sky and names her. In America, so far from his village and his ancestors, Kente

---

40   Gail Godwin. <u>The Good Husband</u> (New York: Ballatine Books, 1994), 467.
41   Alex Haley. <u>Roots</u> (New York: Doubleday, 1974) 343-344.

performs a ritual that he vividly remembers from Africa: "Then, under the moon and stars, Kente raised the baby upward, turning the blanketed bundle in his hands so that the baby's right ear touched against his lips. And then slowly and distinctly, in Mandinka, he whispered three times into the tiny ear, "Your name is Kizzy. Your name is Kizzy. Your name is Kizzy." It was done, as it had been done with all of the Kente ancestors, as it had been done with himself, as it would have been done with this infant had she been born in her ancestral homeland. She had become the first person to know who she was."

Among those who speak Swahili, a child is given a childhood name immediately after birth by a relative of a midwife. Before 40 days pass, the child will be given his or her adult name which is of Islamic or Biblical origin. The child's parents or paternal grandparents name the oldest boy after his paternal grandfather and the oldest girl after her paternal grandmother.

Koreans traditionally assign each person a two-syllable name. The first syllable is the same as his or her siblings and paternal cousins who share the same generation and gender. The syllable has been predetermined for generations and is based on a cycle that in turn is determined by the family's surnames.[42]

In adoption, names can be erased from birth records, lost, changed and combined. Therefore, using names in a meaningful context within the adoption ritual is important. Even when names are changed, the original name, if known, can be incorporated. Telling the origin of names is also an integral part of the ritual as it will promote unity amongst all the families from which the names might stem. If the birthparents and adoptive parents named the child together, that could be explained. If the Korean name of the child is incorporated into the middle name for the child, that process will be stated as an integral part of the ritual.

While a name is something a child carries forever, other important symbols can be used as a theme for a ritual. Appropriate poems and readings can be blended with the symbols to help build a ritual. For instance, kites or balloons work well with a reading of Maureen Connelly's poem:

To Love Something

To love something is to let it go
to allow freedom
to grant space
to be not heavy clouds but gentle winds
to be not the fence but the open path
to be not the lock but the key,
for the greatest of embraces ends with open arms
permitting the ones loved to turn or return as they wish.
This is love. [43]

42   Connie Lockhard. The Melting Pot Book of Baby Names (White Hall, Virginia: Betterway Publications, Inc. 1990) 135.

43   Maureen Connelly, Given in Love (Omaha, Nebraska: Centering Corporation, 1990), 15.

Dr. Seuss's "Oh, the Places You'll Go" works well in any adoption ritual because it speaks to the journey just accomplished as well as the one ahead. Toward the end of Dr. Seuss's book when last names are listed, the family(ies) may opt to personalize the poem by inserting their names, keeping the "Bray" and "O'Shea" for the rhyming.

Oh, the Places You'll Go

On and on you will hike.
And I know you'll hike far
and face up to your problems
whatever they are.
You'll get mixed up, of course,
as you already know.
You'll get mixed up
with many strange birds as you go.
So be sure when you step.
Step with care and great tact
and remember that Life's
a Great Balancing Act.
Just never forget to be dexterous and deft.
And <u>never</u> mix up your right foot with your left.
And will you succeed?
Yes! You will, indeed!
(98 and 3/4 percent guaranteed.)
KID, YOU'LL MOVE MOUNTAINS!

So...
be your name Buxbaum or Bixby or Bray
or Mordecai Ali Van Allen O'Shea,
you're off to Great Places!
Today is your day!
Your mountain is waiting.
So ... get on your way![44]

<hr>

[44]   Dr. Seuss, <u>Oh the Places You'll Go!</u> (New York: Random House, 1990)

The familiar poem by Fleu Conkline Heulinger, "The Answer: To An Adopted Child" could be read. Pink carnations or lilies are traditional symbols of motherhood and relate nicely to this poem.

The Answer: An Adopted Child

Not flesh of my flesh,
nor bone of my bone.
but still miraculously
my own.
Never forget...
for a single minute:
you didn't grow under
my heart,
...but in it.

In conjunction with "The Answer" the poem, "Born Twice" by Imelda Buckley presents the birthmother's perspective in an undisclosed adoption.

Born Twice

You touched me with your smile
I stayed with you awhile
But as I know
You had to go
Through life we both must learn
I'd wandered many a road
And many a spirit glowed
I wanted you
To live anew
To share a family's love
I hope your heart is free
You've grown away from me
You're on my mind
Another time
The pain will pass away
And now I've paid the price
You've really been born twice:
Once with me
The other - free
Into a world of care
Another life has been
Where I could not have seen
She watched you grow
But this I know
We live in unity. [45]

---

45   Used by permission of Patricia Roles. <u>Saying Goodbye to a Baby: The Birthparent's Guide to Loss and Grief in Adoption</u> (Washington, D.C.: Child Welfare League of America, 1989) Volume 1:42-43.

Similarly, the poem "Legacy of an Adopted Child" (author unknown) can hold special meaning, enhanced by carnations or lilies:

Legacy of an Adopted Child

Once there were two women
who never knew each other.
One you do not remember;
the other you call Mother.
Two different lives,
shaped to make yours one.
One became your guiding star;
the other became your sun.
The first gave you life,
and the second taught you to live in it.
The first gave you a need for love,
and the second was there to give it.
One gave you a nationality;
the other gave you a name.
One gave you the seed of talent;
the other gave you an aim.
One gave you emotions;
the other calmed your fears.
One saw your first sweet smile;
the other dried your tears.
One gave you up —
It was all she could do.
The other prayed for a child,
and God led her straight to you.
And now you ask me
through your tears,
the age-old questions
through the years;
heredity or environment —
which are you the product of?
Neither, my darling — neither,
just two different kinds of love.

For a birthparent(s) who are not present, Joannie Liesenfelt's poem, "We Share the Moon" speaks her heartfelt words as a birthmother.[46]

We Share the Moon

We share the moon, you and I.
In the quiet of this night,
a quarter of its light
unfolds over time
till it's whole
like you and I.

The poem works well with a song that many have associated with adoption, "Somewhere Out There."[47] The image of wholes and halves, like the moon in its phases, recognizes that adopted children have missing pieces, particularly when information about birthparents is incomplete.

Therapist Claude Riedel envisions another way to depict each participant in a ritual. Using a bowl filled with water, representing humanity, he suggests that family members contribute a rock to the bowl in a unifying act. In this way, each member, including the newest, is seen to have a place in the larger human family.

In a ceremony adapted from a Preparation for Birth ritual, yarn is used to "connect" a child between the two sets of parents. The birthparents could be represented by proxy if they are not present. Significant people who will contribute to the child's life can be included in the yarn ritual. Once everyone is tied together, the yarn is cut with pieces attached to each participant. The cut yarn represents that the child is a separate person from his/her birth and adoptive parents but carries into life attributes from both sets of parents. The yarn represents a parent's main task, that of raising a child who will form healthy relationships apart from the family.

Addressing the literal aspects of a ritual's content, the purpose of a ritual needs to be clearly stated as the ritual begins. A written prayer can be read or someone can speak about the reasons for holding the ritual. Once the ritual's objective is stated, participants may appreciate a moment of silence to connect with the ritual's purpose at a deeper level.

As adoption advisor, Sally Watson says, "The important thing to remember is that this is the spiritual sealing of the pledge between the birthparents and the adopting parents as they move into the next stage of the relationship... This is an adopted child's most important passage and should be recognized and honored as such."[48]

Once the purpose has been established, the participants can move into the body of the ritual. Providing music for guests to sing would bring people together through a unity of voices. Readings and recitations, such as Dr. Seuss's "Oh, The Places You'll Go!" will bring focus to the many feelings evoked by the ritual. Symbolic actions will draw

---

46   Joannie Liesenfelt. Cold Paper: A Mother's Search for her Daughter. (Downers Grove, Illinois: Cottage Books), 235.
47   See MUSIC on page 78.
48   Used by permission from Pact Press, 3450 Sacramentao Street, Suite 239, San Francisco, California 94118.

attention to the unique journey of adoption for various participants. Gifts that are presented or exchanged will symbolize the adoption journey for the child, mark his/her country or family of origin, and mark the adoption itself.

Grounding the Ritual

The ending of a ritual should be just as intentional as its beginning. Pay attention to ways of bringing closure to feelings and helping all who have attended move away from the ritual and re-enter their world.

This "grounding of a ritual" can be accomplished by finishing some of the tasks that began the ritual: blowing out candles, having a final blessing, singing or playing instruments or having each person greet one another with hugs or handshakes.

After grounding the ritual, participants can move more easily into a time of socializing and eating. Cheryl Flugaur-Leavitt, of RAP, suggests fruit, cheese and bread as a menu. The fruit represents bounty of the earth, and bread is "the staff of life." As a milk product, cheese illustrates human's connection with the animals that comprise our environment. Flugaur-Leavitt feels that the adoptive parents should act as the hosts who feed the guests and personally serve the birthparents if they are present.

A Case for
Repeating Rituals

Some rituals, such as a birthday or anniversary celebration, are repeated annually to target the life's passage. Birthdays are marked by an exchange of gifts and cards or a party theme that centers around the age of the child. In anniversaries, the couple may spend the evening together or even ritualize the event by renewing vows. So too, the significance of an adoption ritual can be repeated on an annual basis by the immediate and extended family. The reminder of that special day may be a fresh time of joy, solidarity and thanksgiving.

Weddings include the phrase "till death do us part," not to inject sadness into a joyous occasion, but to put the ritual into perspective within the continuum of life. While the focus of a repeated adoption ritual should be celebration, be sure to address the loss out of which adoption was born. Otherwise the fullness of the ritual will lose meaning.

In an annual adoption remembrance, the child has the opportunity to understand adoption differently, according to his/her developmental age. At 2 or 3, a child has little insight into adoption and not until pre-school and kindergarten does he/she begin to see that not everyone is adopted. By middle childhood, children begin to grasp the idea that to join one family means leaving another. By the teen years, adopted children explore who they are, both within and outside of adoption. The adoption ritual will address and mark those various passages; the annual remembrance taking on fresh significance with age.

Depending on what stage or what issues of adoption the child is experiencing, the ritual may be harder to repeat some years than others. Adoption rituals, like birthdays, can be dreaded or anticipated, celebrated or just as soon forgotten. Even in the tough years, there are advantages in repeating the ritual.

First, the ritual allows the loss to be spoken aloud and provides an opportunity for healing to occur. Secondly, for all participants, the ritual increases the consciousness of adoption's meaning. Thirdly, the ritual will take on its own life and significance, perhaps never as charged and heightened as with the initial ritual, but still maintaining a sense of continuity through repetition.

Already some adoptive families repeat rituals by celebrating the day that their child joined their family, calling it an Adoption Day or Arrival Day. If the child is internationally or transracially adopted, the event may include elements of his/her native culture. This ritual may include a special cake, an outing, a gift or some reminder to the child of the parents' commitment to him or her. Repetition gives the child an annual sense of significance and importance.

ritualist, marks her children's birthdays with a large candle that has scrollwork. The candle is burned only on the birthday, and the yearly burning is anticipated by her children. In a similar way, adoption could be marked by a candle or keepsake, engraved or designed with appropriate sayings or symbols. A baby pillow, embroidered with a blessing, or a music box are meaningful keepsakes.

The keepsake may be donated by birthparent(s) or designed in their honor. A toy or doll from the birthparent(s)' childhood will be treasured by their birth child in the future. A letter written by a birthparent will also hold special meaning. Particularly in cases where little is known about the birthparents, the keepsake will serve as a physical reminder of those who could not participate physically but still have a symbolic presence in the child's life.

A keepsake may also represent the time, short or long, in which the child was in the care of his or her birthparent(s). Through words or symbols, pay attention to the time before the child was adopted, mentioning birthparents and their ancestry. If jewelry, half of a mitzvah coin, a locket, doll or stuffed animal given by the birthparent is in the child's possession, that article can become a focal point for the ritual. A letter written by a birthparent may be read aloud. In open adoptions, the presence of birthparent(s) completes the ritual.

One adoptive mother did a needlepoint of the alphabet as she waited for her son to arrive from Korea, framing the needlepoint and putting it above her son's crib. Articles that carry such powerful significance will take on a different meaning for her son than for her. Because the needlepoint was symbolic of a time in both their lives, it can be incorporated easily into an adoption ritual.

Presented at the initial ritual, keepsakes and gifts can be put into a special container, much like a menorah or Christmas tree decorations, and retrieved only for the annual ritual.

As children start to understand their adoption ritual, they may choose to add objects like baseball cards or a birds nest they found. Eventually they may design their own symbolic way of expressing how they joined their family. Thirteen-year-old Carrie made a return trip to Columbia, taking a picture of the orphanage in which she had lived and adding that photograph to the ritual.

Nine-year-old Josh decided to draw a family tree with birth family as roots and adoptive family as branches. "This is the family I came from," he said, pointing to the roots, "and this is the family I came to," he said of the branches.

Repeating the ritual allows children to "grow the celebration" as they grow. After a short ceremony he or she may have a pizza feast at age 7, an amusement park outing at age 9 or attend a live theater performance or concert at age 16.

Ritualizing Grief

Grief is a passion to endure.
People can be stricken with it,
victims of it, stuck on it.
Or they can meet it, get through it,
and become quiet victors
through the active, honest, and
courageous process of grieving.
                    Alla Renee Bozarth, Ph.D.[49]

While adoption rituals center on celebration, the grief of birthparents needs to be acknowledged and ritualized. Since adoption is practiced quietly, it is easy to ignore the life-altering decision of birthparents and its impact on their lives. Many times after relinquishment of their child, they move into the shadows, living out their sorrow in silence. Both birthmothers and birthfathers need a way to put words around their loss and to address it in a healing way.

Children who have been uprooted from birth family, foster families, siblings or extended family will be sad about the losses they have incurred. These children may have difficulty adjusting or bonding to their permanent family because they have not been able to fully grieve losing their other families.

Words of peace and consolation need to be said or read in a ritual. The celebrant can do so, and certainly the adoptive family can prepare in advance or speak extemporaneously about their wish for healing for birthparents. A quiet moment of contemplation about birthparents, particularly if they are not present, is also appropriate.

Gerald Manley Hopkins, in his poem "Heaven-Haven" wrote these comforting words:

Heaven-Haven

I have desired to go
Where springs not fail,
To fields where flies no sharp and sided hail
And a few lilies blow.
And I have asked to be
Where no storms come,
Where the green swell is in the havens dumb,
And out of the swing of the sea.

49   Alla Renee Bozarth, Ph.D. <u>Life is Goodbye, Life is Hello: Grieving Well Through All Kinds of Loss.</u> (Minneapolis, Minnesota: CompCare Publishers, 1986) Back Cover.

Since grief is a chronic condition, much music, prose and poetry has been written about the subject. As in Hopkins's poem, the subject matter may not be adoption, but the essence of the writing fits it to the ritual.

The Sacrifice Flower[50]

by Sister Jose Hobday

(Sister Jose Hobday, a Franciscan nun and
Native American, recalls a custom practiced
by her Seneca Iroquois people: the sacrifice flower.)

My mother, who was a native American, taught me all kinds of wonderful ways to pray when I was a child. A very special one was the Sacrifice Flower prayer, which she adapted from the heritage of her people, the Seneca Iroquois.

She taught me to say this prayer when I was feeling low or had a burden I wanted lifted. Later I learned to use it for happy occasions and when I had a special request I wanted to make of God.

Like all mothers, she could always tell when something was bothering me. She'd say to me, "All right, Jo, I think it's time for you to go outside and find yourself a Sacrifice Flower. It's time you get your burden lifted from your heart and give it to God."

So I'd go looking for a flower. Sometimes Mother would go out with me to help me with my flower or talk about what was bothering me. Sometimes, too, she had something weighing on her heart, and she would find a Sacrifice Flower of her own.

The flower was supposed to be special, one that meant a lot to me. As a girl, I picked dandelions, hollyhocks and daisies. So I usually picked one of them. In addition, Mother said I was to be very careful with the flower because it had been selected for a holy purpose. I lovingly cupped it in my hands so nothing would happen to it.

When I got home, I did as my mother instructed and told the flower what burden I wanted lifted and taken to God. How was the flower to do this? Remember, this was a Sacrifice Flower, one that was going to die. The idea was that as life went out of the flower, it would carry my prayer to God.

This meant, of course, the flower was not to be placed in water. I had a shelf in my room that I liked to use for my Sacrifice Flower because it was sort of private, and yet I could see it as I went in and out.

50   Reprinted with permission from <u>Praying</u> Magazine, Box 419335, Kansas City, Missouri 64141.

Every time I saw the flower, I could see it giving its life for me, and I could imagine my prayer being carried to the Lord. That was true even when I was elsewhere and was just thinking about the flower. Either way, I had a strong sense my prayer was being heard. My flower and I were in union.

Sometimes it took a few days, sometimes a couple of weeks. When the flower finally died, I would take it outside, say goodbye to it, and thank it for giving its life for me and for delivering my prayer. Then I would bury it so it would have a chance at a new life, and I always hoped it would come back as an even nicer flower.

In this simple, graphic way my mother taught me how uplifting prayer can be. And, in the process she taught me about life too - how basic both dying and rising are to living and how important it is that we become Sacrifice Flowers for each other.

A Note from the Author

The intent of using the Sacrifice Flower ritual is that it serves as a way to hold one's grief inside a symbol. By doing so, the person can begin to transform that grief, much like the cycles of life do. The flower represents birth, death and rebirth, all of which are elements inherent in rituals. Even though adoption is not a literal death for the birthparents, the loss of the child and giving up the role of being a parent feels like a death to many birthparents. Therefore, the sacrifice flower ritual can help address the grief of losing a child.

*(The following "Adoption Placement Ceremony" is
described by Randolph W. Severson as common
practice in his non- sectarian adoption agency.
Birthparent(s) may or may not be present at these
ceremonies, but are mentioned by name.)[51]*

"Ceremonies at the agency are signaled by the chiming of a bell. With perhaps a little too much overt symbolism, but symbolism in which I take a child's delight, a worker walks the halls with a silver triangle that she gently chimes as a summons to gather in the conference room.

..."As you approach the door, the gentle sounds of a recorded harp will greet you, enchanting the air, gentling the soul and preparing the spirit for the magic of what is about to happen.
..."Although our agency is non-sectarian, we invite the adoptive couple to invite their pastor to participate, to pray or to offer a blessing. Some have boomed glory, some have gently blessed. Some recall the ancient traditions. All remind us that though we have all the virtues we have nothing if we have not love.
"At the front of the room the adoptive parents stand, already with the child.
These words are read — a welcome and a poet's blessing.

An Adoptive Placement Ceremony

On this first day of November, 1991, we are celebrating with Timothy and Elizabeth as they welcome Alexander into their family.

This important and joyous occasion has special meaning for many people. We wish to acknowledge the birthmother, Caitrin, whose love for this baby directed her decision and plan.

We are grateful to the foster parents, John and Michele Jones, and their children, Robert, Michael, Melissa and Joy, who loved and cared for Alexander while he was in their home.

We celebrate with Timothy and Elizabeth, who are assuming the most important role and responsibility of life, that of being parents to a child.

We welcome family members and friends who are here to offer their support to Timothy and Elizabeth, and to share in their happiness of having Alexander join their family.

We at the agency wish your newly expanded family health and happiness. You will share many things as a family; the most important of these is love.

Timothy and Elizabeth, we wish you well in your new vocation as parents of Alexander.
(Then a reading from Kahlil Gilbran's <u>The Prophet</u> is read.)

---

51   Randolph W. Severson. <u>Eyes that Shine: Essays on Open Adoption.</u> (Dallas, Texas: House of Tomorrow Productions, Publication date unknown) 22-24

The Medicine Bag[52]

by Sister Jose Hobday

*(Yet another suggestion for an adoption ritual comes from
Sister Jose Hobday.)*

When children were born in my family, they got a special birth gift. My father made us each a little leather pouch - our own little medicine bag. It was something he had learned from my mother who was a Seneca Iroquois.

My mother put two things in it, and so did my dad. Then they gave the medicine bag to us, and we were to put it in a special place. If you died without your medicine bag, as some of my brothers did during the war, then it was buried separately. Otherwise, the medicine bag was buried with you.

When we got old enough to understand, we were told what was in our medicine bag. One thing my mother put in mine was a pinch of land from the state of Texas.[53] That's because I was born there. Imagine - putting Texas in a bag! She also kept a piece of umbilical cord from my birth, about two inches. She dried it in the sun. Then she put this into the bag, crumbling it into the Texas soil. These two things, the cord and the pinch of Texas, symbolized that I came out of the land and out of my parents. They were to help me remember that I didn't start out by myself, and I was dependent upon the land and upon my family.

My father put a bird feather into each child's medicine bag. He burned a small part of the feather and mixed it in with the things Mother had put in. The reason was that birds were of the sky. They can soar to the horizon and beyond. The feather said that each of us was to soar also and find our place in the world.

None of us ever knew what other item Dad put into our bags. It represented the unknown, the mystery in life. No matter how we tried, he would not tell us. We had our suspicions, and we guessed and guessed, but he would never even give us a hint.

To have a mystery set before me like this early in life proved a big help when I began to work with the mysteries in my life that came along later. It also helped me to understand that God is the center of all mystery.

I still have my medicine bag. It was a wonderful gift from my parents, and it has shown me the importance of making symbols that tie us to places and to people and to God.

---

52   Reprinted with permission from <u>Praying</u> Magazine, Box 419335, Kansas City, Missouri 64141.
53   In international adoption, it is possible for soil to be collected from the child's native country and used in a ritual. Some adoptive parents travel to the child's country to pick up their child and could gather the soil sample then. Or the escort who accompanies the child to their new country could bring the soil.

Although Sister Hobday describes a birth ritual in "The Medicine Bag," the practice can easily be adapted to adoption. A special container can be filled with symbols of the child's birth and homeland, much like a time capsule. Hopes for the future can be included, and of course, items that represent the adoption. The ritual can take place around the gathering and presenting of these items.

Commonly Used Symbols

For designing adoption rituals, both religious and secular,
the following ideas are offered. Included is a discussion of
some of the most often used and referred-to symbols.

CANDLES do more than illuminate with dramatic light. They are universal symbols used by both religious and secular communities. The lighting of a candle has always been highly symbolic and linked with the soul. Candlelight is a powerful symbol to the subconscious mind that something out of the ordinary, and perhaps sacred, is taking place. [54]

— *Birth and adoptive parents can light a candle of unity.*

— *For absent birthparents, a lit candle could represent their light in the child's life.*

— *Each participant can borrow light from a central candle that represents the child. As they light their candle, they may say a wish for the child.*

— *A log can have 3 holes drilled in it to hold 3 candles, one representing birthparent(s), one representing adoptive parent(s) and the other the future of the child.*

— *A candle can be created and inscribed, retrieved yearly for an anniversary ritual.*

JEWELRY has long been exchanged or given as a token of love. Entitlement is shown by jewelry that is bequeathed to an heir, heiress or royalty.

— *Jewelry with birthstones, given by birthparents and/or adoptive parents, can be presented at the ritual to the child and saved for his/her use when they are older.*

— *Birthstones of the child and significant family members are always appropriate additions to jewelry.*

— *Gold represents permanence and happiness that is never marred by time.*

— *Amber holds value for its beauty.* The Magic Amber: A Korean Legend[55] *is a children's story that could be combined with a presentation of amber jewelry.*

---

54   Diane Stein. <u>Casting the Circle A Women's Book of Ritual.</u> (Freedom, California: Crossing Press, 1990) 48.
55   Reasoner, Charles. <u>The Magic Amber: A Korean Legend.</u> (USA: Troll Associates, 1994)

BALLOONS are symbols of hopes and dreams.

— *Build a balloon bouquet with each guest adding a balloon and speaking a wish for the child.*

— *Releasing balloons can be both a liberation of grief and a token of hope for the future.*

ANGELS! The popular revival of ANGELS brings many possibilities for designing a ritual with an angelic theme. Every culture has a tradition of angels that appears in stories, folklore, music and art. Guardians of humans, messengers from the heavens, connectors of those who are parted from one another, angels fit into adoption rituals.

— *When Thomas Carlyle said, "Music is well said to be the speech of angels," he recognized that music and angels go "hand and wing."*

— *A poem that expresses the connection of music and angels is Howard Thurman's* **"Singing of Angels."**

There must be always, remaining in every life, some place or the singing of angels. Some place for that which in itself is breathless and beautiful. Life is saved by the speech of angels.

— *A wonderful music selection is "The Evening Prayer" from Engelbert Humperdinck's opera "Hansel and Gretel." The children sing to evoke their guardian angels to watch over them.*

— *John Donne's* **"Air and Angels"** *contains these lines which could express the feelings of the adoptive and birth family:*

Twice or thrice had I loved thee,
Before I knew thy face or name.
So in a voice, so in a shapeless flame,
Angels affects us oft, and worshipped be.

— *Guardian angel pins can be given to guests to wear. Some are available with a birthstone that could be matched to the child's birth.*

— *Harp music is a lovely addition to an angelic-theme.*

KITES, likewise, soar and reach the heights to which we aspire.

— *The Japanese carp kite symbolizes a son and can be a focal point for a boy's adoption ritual.*

— *The joyful strains of "Let's Go Fly a Kite"* [56] *can add a meaningful musical touch.*

HANDPRINTS and/or FOOTPRINTS are symbols of an indelible moment in time. At our birth, both are recorded as a means of identification. As we pass through life, our feet become our base, and our hands, the means by which we manipulate our living.

— *An adoption ritual can be built around these physical extensions of the child.*

— *A circle of hands can be created through fingerpaint. Place the child's handprint in the middle and imprint a circle of family's hands around the child's.*

— *A reading or calligraphy of Dr. Seuss's "Oh the Places You'll Go" works well with doing a child's footprints that can be framed.*

— *If vows are exchanged, those who make the vows could hold the hand of ones receiving the vows.*

56   See MUSIC chart on page 78.

Cultural Considerations

AFRICA AND AFRICAN AMERICAN — Include the traditional dress of dashikis, kanzus, lappa or bubba and a kofi for the head.

— *Serve fufu from West Africa, chapatis and samusas from East Africa and plantains from both.*[57]

— *Why not combine an adoption ritual with one of these African American holidays, Juneteenth, Junkanoo, Kwanzaa or Harambee?*

— *For an older child, include an activity such as making a drum. Instructions are given in* Kids Explore America's African-American Heritage. *(See Bibliography)*

— *Poetry by Langston Hughes or Maya Angelou is always wonderful.*

— *In Africa, babies are welcomed with songs.*

— *In Zaire, Mbuti babies are passed among a circle of friends who individually greet the baby.*

— *The CD "Deep Forest" has enchanting centuries-old Pygmy chants from central Africa. Included on this CD is "Sweet Lullaby." (Celine Music/Synsound - 1992)*

CHINA - Include paper dragons, kites, bamboo, Chinese herbs, stuffed panda bears and a Chinese vase with flowers.

— *Show a video of traditional Chinese dances or even a nature video of a trip through China.*

— *Have a calligraphy done in Chinese lettering of the child's name. Good wishes for the child can also be done in calligraphy.*

— *Burn incense or feature a potpourri of jasmine, cedar and sandlewood.*

— *Ring a gong to cast the circle and to ground the ritual.*

— *Feasts can include foods from the child's province. Offer chopsticks to guests.*

— *Try reading Chinese nursery rhymes from* Dragon Kites and Dragonflies.[58]

---

57   Recipes are found in Cooking the African Way. Look in the Helpful Resource section.

58   Demi. Dragon Kites and Dragonflies. (New York: Harcourt Brace and Company, 1986).

KOREA - Include the traditional dress, chi'ma and chogori (pale blue skirt and top) or hanbok.

— *A videotape of traditional dances such as the fan dance could be viewed.*

— *Objects such as a fan with the Tanchong symbol for good luck, protection and the cycle of reincarnation could be displayed.*

— *Korean women traditionally deliver their babies on a blanket. A symbolic blanket could represent the birth.*

— *The 100 Day Celebration is a Korean festival that welcomes the baby when he or she is 100 days old. With many guests present, the baby's pictures are prominently displayed and a meal of seaweed soup and rice cakes is served.*

— *In Korea the first birthday is the only birthday besides the sixtieth which is celebrated. At the first birthday celebration the table holds symbols of the child's future: yarn represents long life, money for wealth, a notebook for the child's education. Rice cakes, candy and fruit are served.* [59]

— *Serve mandoo kook (soup with pork dumplings), kim chee, and bulogi or other Korean fare.*

INDIA - Include silks and the traditional sari, stuffed tigers and elephants.

— *Massage is important in Indian culture, particularly a mother massaging her young baby with coconut or diluted mustard oil.*

— *Gold and elaborate jewelry is worn at celebrations in India and can be presented as keepsakes.*

— *An Indian feast might include chapati (flat bread pancake), lentils, dol or a hot spicy curry. Other tasty possibilities are koftas (large meatballs stuffed with hard-boiled eggs)and kheema (ground meat.) Recipes are found in An Invitation to Indian Cooking. (See page 88.)*

LATIN AND SOUTH AMERICA - Include the traditional dress from the country of origin for the child, a poncho, peasant blouse, the Peruvian bowler hat.

— *In Guatemala a child's eighth day of life is celebrated by guests coming to kiss the baby and have a feast. For this occasion candles are lit and the child wears a new outfit.*

— *In Puerto Rico guests arrive for a feast of roast pig, pigeon peas and salad. Each guest is given an encintado or ribbon with the child's name on it.*

— *Why not combine an adoption ritual with a Spanish holiday such as the New Year (El Año Nuevo) or Three Kings' Day (El Día de los Reyês.)*

— *Traditional South and Latin American instruments and dances can enliven the ritual.*

---

59   Margy Burns Knight. Welcoming Babies. (Gardiner, Maine: Tilbury House, 1994), Notes.

PHILIPPINES - The tropical beauty of the Philippines can be demonstrated with bowls of mangoes and papaya as well as hibiscus and bird of paradise flowers.

— *Show a video of traditional Filipino dancing such as the tinikling, performed with two bamboo poles.*

— *Amulets are presented as protective symbols to babies in the Philippines.*

— *Traditional foods include adobo (pickled pork or chicken), cascaron (coconut donuts), lumpia (fried beef rolls), enseimada (sweet rolls), and pancit (fried noodles.)*

— *A tree is often planted where the umbilical cord was buried.*

— *Even without an umbilical cord, a symbolic planting of a tree in honor of the child's birth could be accomplished.*

VIET NAM - A 100 Day Celebration welcomes the baby when he or she is 100 days old. The angels that cared for the child and kept him or her safe are thanked at this ritual.

— *Many articles are placed on a table that represent occupations such as a pen, a hammer and a paintbrush. If the child touches any one of these articles, it is considered an omen of his/her future occupation.*

Note from the Author

Why not create your own object or theme-based ritual from rainbows, moon and stars, ribbons, dream-catchers, origami or the seasons. From any one season a ritual could be built around spring flowers and renewal, summer warmth and growth, autumn leaves and change, or winter's time of slumber and hibernation.

Music

Background music can add warmth and suggest contentedness. Music from the child's culture or country of origin can represent that child's roots.

Adoptive parents and birthparents could sing a round, beginning and ending at various times to represent their intersecting roles in the child's life.

Lullabies are always appropriate:

— *"Lullaby (Goodnight, My Angel)" - Billy Joel on "River of Dreams" album/CD*

— *"Hush, Little Baby" is a playful lullaby that lists many gifts, concluding with the parents' love being the most lasting gift. For a more playful version of this lullaby, Bobby McFerrin joins with Yo-Yo Ma on the CD/Album "Hush."*

— *"Mighty Like a Rose"*

— *"For Baby (For Bobbie)" by John Denver Copyright 1965 Cherry Lane Music. (On "Album," Peter Paul and Mary)*

Other musical selections might include:

— *"From A Distance" Julie Gold; Julie Gold Music Publishing. Also sung by Bette Midler on "Experience the Divine" album/CD*

— *"Let's Go Fly A Kite" - Richard M. Sherman and Robert B. Sherman, Wonderland Music Company.*

— *"Simple Gifts" is a Shaker hymn of simplicity that may be sung.*

— *In "Appalachian Spring" Aaron Copland wrote variations of the Shaker Tune. "Appalachian Spring" can be found on the CD/cassette recording of "The Joy of Bernstein."*

— *"Somewhere Out There" James Horner, Barry Mann, Cynthia Weil.*

— *"Sunrise Sunset" from "Fiddler on the Roof."*

— *"Wind Beneath my Wings" - Larry Henley & Jeff Silbar; WB Gold Music Corporation. Also sung by Bette Midler on "Experience the Divine" album/CD.*

— *"Everybody Wins" (A song about open adoption that addresses the affection and special bond between birth and adoptive parents.) Steve and Ellen Seskin. Write Steve Seskin, P.O. Box 2362, Richmond, CA 94803-1362.) Sung by Steve and Ellen Seskin on "Life's A Dance" CD.*

— *"He Would Be Sixteen" Michelle Wright sings a birthmother's song by Jill Colucci, Charlie Black and Austin Roberts. Available on "Now & Then" through Arista Records.*

African and African-American music might include:

— *"Loop de Loo"*

— *"Little Sally Walker"*

— *"Fais Do Do, Colas" (Sung in Patois)*

— *"All the Pretty Little Horses"*

— *"I will Feed my Baby" (Yoruba)*

— *"Kumbaya" was originally a lullaby in the Congo. For lullaby words see <u>Shake It To the One You Love The Best: Play Songs and Lullabies from Black Musical Traditions</u>. (See page 88.)*

Readings and Words Spoken
from the heart

— *The birthparents may hold the child in a blanket and reflect on the child's birth and life. Whatever is spoken can be also presented in written form as a gift that stays with the child, but is shared with those in attendance.*

— *Names are vital in adoption. Naming ceremonies focus on this aspect of identity. Even in other adoption rituals, reciting names and telling their meaning can be a focal point of the ritual.*

— *Poems that celebrate and contemplate adoption are helpful inclusions. (See Bibliography) Perspectives on a Grafted Tree included many adoption poems.*

— *In Japan's Shinto religion, prayers are written on slips of papers that are tied to trees. Special wishes and blessings could be tied to branches of a tree or a branch brought into the ritual.*

Keepsakes and Gifts

— *A birth family tree can be developed and framed with medical, family and other information about heritage. The tree could be framed and given to the child for his/her room.*

— *Likewise, a family tree of the adoptive family could be framed to hang beside the birth family tree.*

— *Either birth or adoptive families could present a blanket at the ritual. The birthparent(s) might wish to keep a blanket in which the child rested, or they might want the blanket to go with the child. The blanket can symbolize protection and nurturing on both sides.*

— *An Entrustment Certificate written in calligraphy with ornate lining could include the signatures of all present. Perhaps the inscription could read: "Everybody wanted the best for me at this time in my life."*

— *A Birth Gift could be filled with aspects of the child's life. (See Medicine Bag on page 70.) You may want to include soil from the child's place of birth and other symbols that express wishes for the child.*

Flowers, Herbs and Trees

Throughout human history, flowers, plants and trees have been so interwoven with daily life that they've developed into symbols, sentiments, passions and affections, beliefs and religions, fear and superstitions.[60]

In rituals a bouquet of flowers and herbs can be exchanged between families. They may comprise a potpourri that represents a child's culture. A crown of flowers can by placed on a child, or flowers can be strewn about by younger guests to "cast the circle." A wreath of flowers could be a welcoming gift for the adoptive family or a transition gift for the birth family.

Flowers used in a ritual can be dried for a keepsake.

Below are traditional meanings associated with flowers and various other plants:

Flowers

Carnation, pink	*Symbol of mother-love*
Daisy	*Gentleness and innocence*
Dogwood	*Love in adversity*
Forget-me-not, yellow-blue	*True love, Faithful love and undying memory*
Heliotrope	*Eternal love and admiration*
Honeysuckle, yellow	*Bonds of love*
Iris	*Three petals symbolize faith, wisdom and valor.*
Ivy, green	*Friendship, fidelity*
Jasmine, white	*Transports of Joy*
Lilac, purple	*First emotions of love*
Lilac, white	*Youthful innocence, purity, sweetness*
Lily	*Sacred flower of motherhood*
Lily of the valley, white	*Return of happiness*
Lotus	*Sacred to Eastern religions; Symbol of beauty, perfection and purity because the blossom grows clean out of the muddy pool from which it rises.*
Magnolia, white	*Dignity, perseverance*
Orchid, all colors	*Beauty, magnificence*
Rose, any color	*Love*
Rose, single pink	*Simplicity*
Violet, blue	*Faithfulness*
Zinnia, all colors	*Thoughts of absent friends*

---

60   Ernst Lehner. <u>Folklore and Symbolism of Flowers, Plants and Trees.</u> (New York: Tudor Publishing Company, 1960), 12.

Herbs

Borage	*Courage*
Camomile	*Energy in adversity*
Coriander	*Hidden merits*
Clove	*Dignity and restraint*
Lavender	*Constancy and loyalty*
Marjoram	*Comfort and Consolation Rosemary Remembrance.*
Thyme	*Courage and Activity*

The Sacrificial Flower (See Page 67.)

Trees

Trees are useful symbols for rituals; they reflect the seasons, serving as symbols of strength and often outlasting the humans who planted them. Return to a childhood home and examine the trees as proof of how they serve as markers of the passage of time.

Branches, leaves and twigs from various trees can be singled out for their symbolic connection to the ritual.

Planting a tree, particularly a grafted tree, can be a marker of the adoption. The grafted tree, like an adopted child, receives its essence from two families.

Ash	*Tree of life (Nordic)*
Bamboo	*Durability and longevity (China)*
	Candidness and Devotion (Japan)
Banana	*Birth and Life tree of the Tropics*
Evergreen	*Eternity*
Fig	*Peace and abundance*
Oak	*Stability and Hospitality*
Palm	*Sacred to both Christians and Jews, the palm is a symbol of triumph over adversity.*

Foods

Many rituals are followed by feasts, not just for socializing but as a symbolic gesture of the celebration of life.

— *Native foods from the child's country of origin are a must in the menu for an internationally adopted child. Inviting grandparents to help cook these dishes will bring them into the ritual. (See the Bibliography for cookbooks that feature cultural dishes.)*

— *Cakes decorated with a theme or a saying can grace the table. An older child will enjoy blowing out candles on the cake.*

Summary

RELIGIOUS RITUALS which celebrate and acknowledge the uniqueness of adoption need to be developed and broadened within the religious community. Inclusion of birthparents, by proxy, physical presence or with a special mention, is vital to the ritual.

The purpose of a religious adoption ritual is to:

— *validate adoptive families and birth families within congregations*

— *help congregants support the families*

— *help each participant in the adoption better understand and affirm their new role*

— *mark the passage of the child into their new family.*

Useful ceremonies from various religious traditions include an Entrustment Ceremony, Naming Ceremony for a Baby Girl, Baby Dedication and Thanksgiving for the Gift/Adoption of a Child.

Adoption finalizations can also be ritualized. For older children who are adopted, rituals can be therapeutic and assist them to view their new family as permanent and secure.

SECULAR RITUALS, although difficult to define, incorporate less traditional rhetoric and more creative uses of symbols, objects and music. Both religious and secular ritualists may borrow from other cultures and traditions, or they may borrow from one another.

What is important is that the ritual be meaningful within the context of the various participants' beliefs.

Elements to include in a secular ritual are:

— *A leader or celebrant*

— *An appropriate setting*

— *Gifts to exchange or give, gifts which mark the child's country or family of origin and/or gifts which mark the adoption*

— *Literal and symbolic content*

— *A grounding of the ritual before its closure.*

A strong case exists for repeating adoption rituals throughout the child's adoption and for ritualizing grief and loss. Symbols which can be of use include candles, jewelry, balloons, kites, handprints, footprints and angels. For transracially and internationally adopted children, cultural considerations are an integral part of the ritual.

Whether secular or religious, adoption rituals hold great promise and are filled with long-lasting purpose for those who choose to participate.

Bibliography

Beck, Renee. *The Art of Ritual*. Berkeley, California: Celestial Arts, 1990.

The Book of Common Prayer. New York: The Church Hymnal Corporation and Seabury Press, 1977.

Bozarth, Alla Renee, Ph.D. *Life is Goodbye, Life is Hello: Grieving Well Through All Kinds of Loss*. Minneapolis, Minnesota: CompCare Publishers, 1982.

Campbell, Joseph. *The Power of Myth*. New York: Doubleday, 1988.

Catholic Household Blessings and Prayers. Washington, D.C.: Bishops' Committee on the Liturgy, 1988.

Connelly, Maureen. *Given In Love*. Omaha, Nebraska: Centering Corporation, 1990.

DeGidio, Sandra. *Enriching Faith Through Family Celebrations*. Mystic, Connecticut: Twenty-Third Publications, 1989.

Demi. *Dragon Kites and Dragonflies*. New York: Harcourt Brace and Company, 1986.

Fahlberg, Vera I., M.D. *A Child's Journey Through Placement*. Indianapolis, Indiana: Perspectives Press, 1991.

Godwin, Gail. *The Good Husband*. New York: Ballatine Books, 1994.

Griffith, Keith C. *The Right To Know Who You Are*. Ottawa, Ontario: Katherine C. Kimball, 1991.

Haley, Alex. *Roots*. New York: Doubleday, 1974.

Hobday, Sister Jose. "The Medicine Bag." *Praying Magazine*. 28, (1988) 39.

Hobday, Sister Jose. "The Sacrifice Flower." *Praying Magazine*. 49, (1989): 48-49.

Hochman, Anndee. *Everyday Acts and Small Subversions*. Portland, Oregon: Eighth Mountain Press, 1994.

Jewett, Claudia. *Adopting the Older Child*. Harvard, Massachusetts: Harvard Common Press, 1978.

Johnston, Patricia Irwin. *Perspectives on a Grafted Tree*. Fort Wayne, Indiana: Perspectives Press, 1982.

Knight, Margy Burns. *Welcoming Babies*. Gardiner, Maine: Tilbury House, 1994.

Liesenfelt, Joannie. *Cold Paper: A Mother's Search for Her Daughter*. Downers Grove, Illinois: Cottage Books, 1992.

Lockhard, Connie. *The Melting Pot Book of Baby Names*. 2nd Edition. White Hall, Virginia: Betterway Publications, Inc., 1990.

Margolis, Vivienne. *FanFare For A Feather*. San Jose, California: Resource Publications, Inc., 1991.

Melina, Lois Ruskai and Sharon Kaplan Roszia. *The Open Adoption Experience*. New York: Harper Perennial, 1993.

Reasoner, Charles. *The Magic Amber: A Korean Legend*. USA: Troll Associates. 1994.

Riggs, R.M. *The Minister's Service Book*. Springfield, Missouri: Gospel Publishing House. 1995.

Roles, Patricia. *Saying Goodbye to a Baby: The Birthparent's Guide To Loss and Grief in Adoption*. Volume 1. Washington D.C.: Child Welfare League, 1989.

Seuss, Dr. *Oh, The Places You'll Go!* New York: Random House, 1990.

Severson, Randolph W. *Eyes That Shine: Essays on Open Adoption*. Dallas, Texas: House of Tomorrow Productions. 1992.

Stein, Diane. *Casting the Circle: A Women's Book of Ritual*. Freedom, California: Crossing Press, 1990.

Strassfeld, Michael and Sharon Strassfeld. *The Second Jewish Catalog*. Philadelphia: The Jewish Publication Society of America, 1976.

Tellushkin, Rabbi Joseph. *Jewish Literary: The Most Important Things to Know about the Jewish Religion, Its People, and Its History*. New York: William Morrow and Company, Inc., 1991.

United Church of Christ (U.C.C.) Order of Worship. Princeton, New Jersey: Consultation on Church Union.

van Gulden, Holly and Lisa M. Bartels-Rabb. *Real Parents, Real Children: Parenting the Adopted Child.* New York: The Crossroad Publishing Company, 1993

Williamson, Gay and David. *Transformative Rituals: Celebrations for Personal Growth*. Deerfield Beach, Florida: Health Communications, Inc., 1994.

Ethnic Recipes

Harrison, Supeen and Judy Monroe. _Cooking the Thai Way_. Minneapolis, Minnesota: Lerner Publications Co., 1986.

Jaffrey, Madhur. _An Invitation to Indian Cooking_. New York: Vintage Books Edition. 1975.

Nabwire, Constance and Bertha Vining Montgomery. _Cooking the African Way_. Minneapolis, Minnesota: Lerner Publications Co., 1988.

Wolfe, Robert L. and Diane. _Cooking the South American Way_. Minneapolis, Minnesota: Lerner Publications Co., 1991.

Yoon, Moon Ja. _Korean Cooking for You_. Seoul, Korea: Seoul Press, 1992.

Resources For African-American Projects

Mattox, Cheryl Warren. _Shake it to the One That you Love the Best: Play Songs and Lullabies from Black Musical Traditions._ Nashville, Tennessee: JTG of Nashville, 1989.

Westridge Young Writers' Workshop. _Kids Explore America's African-American Heritage._ Santa Fe, New Mexico: John Muir Publications, 1993.

Other Helpful Resources

RAP–Resources for Adoptive Parents
    3381 Gorham Avenue
    Minneapolis, Minnesota 55426   *In Minnesota Only (800) 944-5230*
                                   (612) 926-6959

RAP's mission is to inform, support and advocate for families touched by adoption. Located in Minneapolis, RAP provides support for parents and children, respite care at a camp setting, educational workshops/meetings and a lending library. RAP support groups address the unique issues of adoption, regardless of a child's age at placement or the cultural heritage of children and parents.

AFA (Adoptive Families of America)
    333 Highway 100 North
    Minneapolis, MN 55422
    For merchandise orders/magazine subscriptions (800) 372-3300.
AFA provides problem-solving assistance and information about the challenges of adoption as well as many adoption-related products. Many of the books suggested in Designing Rituals of Adoption for the Religious and Secular Community are available through AFA. "Adoptive Families" Magazine is published 6 times a year.

ALMA (Adoptees' Liberty Movement Association)
    PO Box 154
    Washington Bridge Station
    New York, New York 10033   *(212) 581-1568*
    ALMA provides a network of understanding, compassion and information to adopted persons.

Child Welfare League of America
    440 First Street NW, Suite 310
    Washington D.C. 20001-2085   *(202) 638-2951*
    The Child Welfare League provides a clearinghouse for counseling resources and adoption agencies.

Centering Corporation
    1531 N. Saddle Creek Rd.,
    Omaha, NE 68104   *Phone (402) 553-1200*
                                   FAX: (402) 553-0507
The Centering Corporation has many resources for addressing grief including birthparent grief. "With Courage and Love: A Birthmother's Journal" and "Given in Love" was designed for birthmothers.

Concerned United Birthparents (CUB)
    2000 Walker Street
    Des Moines, IA 50317   *(515) 263-9558*
    CUB is a national organization with local chapters that offers support, advocacy and information to birthparents.

Cottage Books and Joannie Liesenfelt have created a collection of poems, "Cold Paper: A Mother's
  Search for Her Daughter" which traces Liesenfelt's heartfelt journey as a birthmother. Available
  from:
  Cottage Books
  Joannie Liesenfelt
  P.O. Box 9276
  Downers Grove, IL 60515

National Adoption Information Clearinghouse
  11426 Rockville Pike, Suite 410
  Rockville, MD 20852   (301) 231-6512
  NAIC provides information on adoption as well as referral services to therapists and other
  professionals.

National Federation for Open Adoption Education
  391 Taylor Blvd. Suite100
  Pleasant Hill, California 94523   (510) 827-2229
  The National Federation for Open Adoption Education provides education and training in
  open adoption for families and professionals.

The National Resource Center for Special Needs Adoption
  16250 Northland Drive, Suite 120
  Southfield, MI 48075   (801) 443-7080
  The National Resource Center for Special Needs Adoption informs adoption professionals and
  advocates of the Center's various activities which includes new developments in the field of
  special needs adoption. "The Round Table" is the Center's newsletter.

North American Council on Adoptable Children (NACAC)
  970 Raymond Avenue #106
  St. Paul, MN 55114-1149
  NACAC organizes adoptive parent support groups, monitors federal child-welfare legislation
  and helps families who have adopted children with special needs.

PACT: An Adoption Alliance
  3315 Sacramento Street, Suite 239
  San Francisco, CA 94118   (415) 221-6957
                                Espanol (415) 221-8765
  PACT is national organization which helps American-born children of color find permanent,
  nurturing, culturally-competent homes. PACT provides packets of information to birth and
  adoptive parents. PACT Press explores many adoption issues through their newsletter.

RESOLVE, Inc.
  1310 Broadway
  Somerville, MA 02144   (617) 623-0744
  Resolve is a national organization of support and information for those affected by infertility.

About the Author

As an adopted person and adoptive mother, Mary Martin Mason frequently writes and speaks at national conferences about adoption issues. She is the author of <u>The Miracle Seekers: An Anthropology of Infertility</u> and <u>Out of the Shadows: Birthfather's Stories.</u> Through her company, Adoptapes, she produces audio and videotapes about adoption. Mason is a board member of Adoptive Families of America, Inc. and is a former executive director of Resolve of the Twin Cities. Her monthly column for a Twin Cities community newspaper has won several awards. Mason resides in a suburb of Minneapolis with her husband, Douglas and son, Joshua.

About RAP (Resources for Adoptive Parents)

RAP's mission is to inform, support and advocate for families touched by adoption. Located in Minneapolis, RAP provides support for parents and children, respite care at a camp setting, educational workshops/meetings and a lending library. RAP support groups address the unique issues of adoption, regardless of a child's age at placement or the cultural heritage of children and parents.

In Minnesota only, call   *(800) 944-5230*
Otherwise call   *(612) 926-6959*
3381 Gorham Avenue
Minneapolis, MN 55426